Acknowledgments

I wish to thank my children for the beautiful presence they add to my life. For the compassion you gave so freely, at a time when life was not so forgiving. For the fortitude and strength you forced me to muster, as a parent, when the easier version, was to simply give up. You three are truly, my most divine works of art, as you each add a palette of color to my life daily. I will love you always.

To my book designer, for all the edits and revisions, and finally *Folds of Flesh*.

To the readers of www.LillianJade.com, as some days the amount of hits on my page was truly inspirational. Life's renderings have never so easily spilled onto paper, as turning fifty years old finally gave me the courage to be the person I was always meant to be. You have all helped in prodding me to embrace my passion for writing words that paint a picture, tell a story, unfold a character, tell of a life, or depict the serenity of poetic verse.

Thank you to any and all I have left out, family and friends, as each of you are part of my journey.

Lillian Jade

Running
is
meditative nourishment
for the soul

Preface

For every writer, every runner, if she or he
is lucky, comes one beautiful idea, together imagi-
native, real, serene, forever establishing with
subject, together, in the firmament of a story.
Transfixed through my sneakers, my firmament,
my master thesis, is a life long course.

Running, always has been an outlet to step
away from everyone else's agendas, and the tug-
ging at me of past history. Weaving through cycles,
life's changes, and loss.

On most mornings as the sweat liberally drips
on my bedroom rug, I am already clicking away at
my keyboard with journal notes, before I even grab
a glass of consoling water. Journals, traditionally
keep track of thoughts and ideas, categorizing
them, as this one begins, I am nearing the fifty
year old benchmark, sad, but true. Falling most
willingly into creative dialogue, as all of me strips
away with the wind, leaving mostly flesh exposed.
The color palette of my life makes for the most
intriguing watercolors, as words spill out along the
pavement or wooded trail, etched across the laces
of my sneakers. The air on my skin, the sensuality
of my movements, the audience of deer, as they
lock eyes with me in darted motion. The strain of
ligaments in silent pose, as a haze of blood streams
through my veins against the vibration of my

heart, all coated in perfusion of a salt laden crust.

In my runs I am insipidly entranced, stripped of all posture and pretense. Absorbed in the arduous comprehension of the passage of time, the inevitability of death, and the ruthless onslaught of the wrought of it all. Accepting that the meaning of life is that eventually, it ends, for all of us, without pride or prejudice as to our walk of life. The in between time is ours to mold, with clarity and decisive decision, we each choose the path of our feet and the paint we color.

In a matter of months I had suffered an accident, multiple reconstructive surgeries, a stroke, amnesia and watched as my brother withered away from the cancer he had just been diagnosed with. A raging sea ran through him, as the waters rose, as the tide rushed in, as the cancer ravaged his body. My amnesia state, the stroke having been suffered, was a wall of a prison I could not break through.

My recovery deemed a long shot, at best, beginning to end, over many barren months, holding my life by a thread, in an attempt to weave together threads of who I was. My brother finally succumbing to the thread of cancer, as I willingly fell into triggers of grief, snapshots of reality tinged with the smell of day old surgical blood.

Life, for me, fell short, in palpable weakness.

In a darkened moment of doubt, an almost hurried second, I think I may have grabbed God's hand. A safe place to say what I needed to say, moving forward from the pain.

Just when I thought I was weak, my sneakers taught me, perhaps, I was the strongest one of all. Battled, but intact, my body began to repair itself, as I learned how to once again become my biggest advocate in a world that had changed so abruptly for me.

Logging the miles. Coasting along the shore, deserted paths, wooded trails, as mile after mile of beaded sweat broke free on my brow. Etching out words in poetic raw succession, I became imposingly bare, down to my flesh.

Loosing all thought to the wind, my overheated body colliding with early morning air, part beginning and end of holding onto me. A Journal in the year of a journey, which, in truth, never does have an end, until the succumbing of my last final breath, many miles from now.

Lillian Jade

Flesh

Rising from the blackest hours of dawn, I step into the steamy shower of my sweat. In a gesture of polite refusal, I wipe away a body drip hanging closest to my lips. Much of my thought negotiated in purest silence. A leaf from a near bare tree topples onto a streetlamp in echo of silent vibration across my breast. Flirting with a bird, flesh liberated in unfamiliar heat, wandering down the back of my thigh, an intrusive sympathetic shudder of morning chill. Something loosens inside of me, as I catch my breath in a lingering send-off of my sneakers.

Lulled by the infatuate hum of
the rain, my sweat hangs on my tongue,
like drops of whiskey I feel their burn.
Tumbling endlessly into rain soaked
thought in drunken stupor, birds mimic a
dance of disappointed lovers. Part of my
breath parts my brain, falling through
my body, coursing through my lungs like
an unwanted intruder, spillage left on
the pavement. As my feet unfold in
exploratory rest, I crumble... sneakers
compress into compliance of their own
will, as I position my feet under the
blanket of my body, wet flesh springing
into trails of goose bumps.

Embers of my smoke escape my
nostrils, as flesh unfolds in nude
sensation, trees reaching down to me
in panic in covering nakedness I am
exposing. The opening of sky, my place
of concentration, sweat runs along the
inner of my thigh. Asking nothing of me,
sneakers competently lead me. Colors

fan out from the center of the sky, inclusive of the paint chips of a new day. Fantasies begin as the paint spills amber and gold across the sidewalk.

Running dialogue with my sneakers, my body channels into different times and places. Sunrays aim straight toward me in an invasion of black swans on the coolest of my flesh. A hollow heard from my ribcage echoes out my spine, as a shiver travels in disguise under the prickling of goose bumps on my forearm. My pink tongue is lolling on beads of cold perspiration, as flesh becomes a paintbrush wet, glistening in the chill of October air.

In a single hurried tug, I willingly surrender to the rain. Direct side way beams of my breast peer out from the drenched skin of my shirt. Sweat works its way methodically downstream, anchoring in my navel. My tongue holding the vibration of breath against my inner cheek, the parade, the dance of my feet moving downhill. Flood gates of damp gray sky open onto my shoulders, length of my legs, running a river down my tailbone. Wet sensation colliding with the rain...

Feeling myself falling on the temptation of sweat, air sliced to an almost translucent thinness falls crisp and brilliant on my lips. A leaf topples falling soundlessly onto my shoulder; its hush seems deeper than my own breathing. An illicit pleasure, smuggled into privation, soft pink clay of my body, soft to the touch. My body's toxins ease the lightening of the burden, as each droplet relieves the chaos left behind, a puddle spreads outward on the pavement. Each leaf falling strums my breath, leaving an imprint on my flesh.

A storm surges beneath my skin, as I inhale crushed red pepper allowing its heat to inflate my flesh. Chilean red pierces my pores; beneath the stone slate of morning sky my muscles twitch at the sound of my pulse thundering in my ears. Honey amber recognition of sun, for today, is forgotten, as dank unused places escort my sneakers.

The rain, acts as my cloak, coverage of my nakedness, winding its way around my body in lovers temperance. Silk white gowns from clouds drape down to dress me in conservatory. The music of my breath is the only rhythm that plays in the background, as sweat drips down in dance across my breastbone.

Nighttime affairs left in darkness
of coal, as morning layers cool and
crisp on my cheek. Angels push on
my shoulders, tasting on my kiss,
succumbing to vibrations in my throat,
as breath out feels the aliveness of
flesh. My hand travels down my careen,
whisking body dew of unforeseen places.
A blood thirst howl from deep inside
my bloodstream echoes now, against
the bark of hardened trees, thoughts
of winter's forthcoming. Sin pools
in deep ravens in my sneakers, persuading
the path of my feet to head east,
not west.

Morning sprouts jelly and jam;
currant, blackberry, apricot colored
leaves imprint on my flesh. My demure,
hidden behind a heavy fortified gate, as
my bareness needs no justification. Skin
flawless, as each step of my sneaker
brings me closer to my rawness. My
body submissive under the adhesive of

sweat, as breasts and shoulders stand at attention.

Subdued...

In darted motion, hedonistic affair between mornings air and last nights darkness. Antiquated inhibitions left curbside, as my sneakers release secrets my flesh had been hiding. Submerging, naked, in a deluge of salted sweat carved in an effortless mural on my back. Hypnotic effect of breath pulsates the copper walls of my bloodstream. Euphoria, in my sneakers, as a love affair entrances me in the seducing of my own body, rivers explode from my cavities, sweat dribbles in swallows of need down my legs.

Unpretentious intrigue floats among the trees, stripping from covers, heat now on my flesh. Picking up pace, as my breath flashes a pickled spice across my shadow on the pavement. Seduced and refined, drinking on my own taste, heeding body's movements.

The poetic blank ribbon of sky seduces both my breath and flesh. My feet infuse with timeless elegance, encouraging me to languish on my sweat. My composition, executed in brushstrokes of color, crimson rose circulates my veins in solicitude.

Everybody needing to go to heaven, as I place my feet in running stride, I am already there. Sneakers, running dialogue with thought, as a rush of sensation erupts from quiet repose of my organs. My blood takes on the color of every rainbow I have ever seen; every sunset my eyes have taken rest upon, every arousal and flush burning need of my animal. I close my eyes behind the blindfold of the sun, letting myself sensually ride a

a Caribbean beach, half naked,
and snow crabs beneath my feet.
On my flesh, the border between the
cool crisp air, and adult – only secrets
pouring out from within. I linger...

My self-portrait hangs amid the
fresh chill of empty air. My body raucous
and unpredictable in a theatrical melting
of my canvas, I unconsciously mirror
the posture of the deer. Crossing onto
a field of silk, a touch of breath,
culminating in the determination of
flesh, blood, and sweat, relaxing of my
spine, just enough to float. A jolt of
energy purrs through me, in an orgasmic
euphoria, as sneakers sidestep in a dance
of morning ritual.
    Perfect symmetry of the moment, as
I stay within the sound of my pumping
heart, relentless tire, as my body's honey
coats the tiny hairs of my covered flesh,
in appreciative eye of a passing stranger.
Sneakers in sudden shyness...

I stand at the edge of another tidal river, the quenching of my navel, as it becomes the teacup for the river of my sweat. Sipping on sounds of my body as lungs fill with air. Lingering for a moment, on this terra firma, folding my body into an arrow of hunger as I plunge downhill. A bird rises in the air, on a small quiver of my stolen breath. Shedding some part of self, as I brush up against a horizon unmarred by my own bareness.

Remembering who I really am, not runner, nor writer, but an animal reveling on the opening of the sun, the sway of the trees, a chord of my scarlet chilled flesh. Granite thoughts toss back my salty mist. My breasts, now holding the slightest of winter's chill, a reminder of what is to come.

Columns of suppressed morning fog simmer within, in an almost audible breath, as sensation drives down my ribcage. I believe frozen raspberries float through my bloodstream, as a meringue of release emerges from my every pore. My body's moment of ultimate cohesion, as emphatic sweat begins to drain, trailing down the curvature of my tailbone, in a dance of tormented sexual persuasion.

The sky, as a silver charcoal, delivers a moment of elegant interlude, leaving tastings on my lips. Forbearance of my sneaker taps at the illusion.

Feeling the heat of my body rise, as flesh presses through my navel, a backward entrance into a silent breathing. Enjoying the meandering trajectory of blood flow, as a band of happy nomads bubbles from my pores, skin refusing to absorb, in a moment of morning lust.

Climbing the hill, meeting the glass full force, breaking and entering,

as liquid gold perfusion streams
from broken shard of sky. Gazing out,
impassive, sailing on a riptide of silence,
patterned waves resolve into my profile.
Flesh enticed by a raw ridge of cool
crisp morning air.

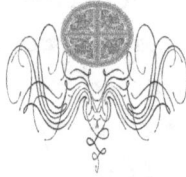

An adrenaline reserve pools from
the foam of my breath, leaving jagged
streams along my arm. Ornate points
of my breast erect in a formal greeting
with the sun gods. A sluggish river of
pretension pours from my shoulders,
as chilled air rearranges itself against
the soft ravine of my spine. Dropping
soundlessly onto the pavement, the
hushed wake of my sneakers.

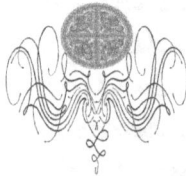

My skin and bones wrap around me as a
venomous snake I choose not to escape.

Dampness lodges in my throat, as I fight back the onset of sudden sweat, around my hips, the stride opens up to a straddling of body arousal. In full camouflage of the foliage, I pretend to be someone else. The smell of the air feels complicated, as it fills my senses with an urgency toward pure abandonment. Like a wild animal against the opening of the autumn sun, I run on layers of silence spread throughout the woods. A cobweb imposes on my flesh...

My sneakers mirroring the split of my own indecision, turn right, or sway left? Birds talk about me in the third person, as I confuse them as the resident bohemian/ intellectual today in the woods. My run becomes my illicit pleasure smuggled in under the opening of the sun.

Mid autumn breeze arriving on my nose, setting a tear in motion at the corner of my eye. Crisp air fringing on the soldiers now piercing through my sports bra. My architectural columns today, one of total erection, as I stand parallel to the groping of the trees. Cold air on my flesh, hot sweat of my breath, both deliver a river of collision traveling around my navel.

Hurdling an archipelago, my sneakers drown in a puddle, drunk on rain and adrenaline, tantalizingly liberating to my undercurrent. A subtle aura of my honeysuckles wafts in the wind.

My sneakers float me, air imprints on my flesh, molding, as if I were made of soft clay.

My body reading all the messages delivered by the sun, as I lay like a goddess, interpreting the chirping of the birds.

Balancing the active and the passive, the tuning in and the letting go. Rising into an embrace with the gold of the sun; following sound into silence. The stream of pulse and breath, now meet as two rivers... as I nakedly plunge into the depths of the waters.

Sun glinting on my shoulders, thin veil of cloud reaches down to poke at my undergrowth. Stained glass of the sky reaches the black and white marble of the pavement, backdrop for my sweat. Soft spot between my hips and navel releases on each step.

Deer look on in awkwardness at my forbidden. The river of my blood coarsely pumping through each minuscule vein, sneakers delivering that all-inclusive potion sending endorphins of self derived opiate to my brain. Sprinkles of my salt languish on my tongue, as I lick the dew from my shoulder blade.

Muffled silence of the trees slides

along the edge of my jaw, framed in beads of perspiration. Walls of my lungs bend outward to contain my breath, settling to a steady sway from a quiet breeze blowing against my upper lip.

Falling into the run, letting myself perilously wash away. Rain touches lightly at the back of my neck, chancing that it might find me aloft in a dream. Waiting until my breathing deepens, then grows quiet, tatting of my own flesh, a flavor of heightened anticipation. My thin substance weaves in and out beneath the trees. There is no one here to give me caution, my blood pulsating in ostentation.

Feeling the mud on my shin, letting it imprint on my flesh, warm and demanding as its murkiness fills my senses. Stone lined garden spaces grace the space between my hipbones, as the tiniest veil of vines drips down my leg. Sweat drapes from my brow, precipitous drop of despair, feeling the strain in the deepest of places.

A river of puddles washes over my sneaker; as my own river of wetness, adds to the drowning. A fallen leaf floats away, on a single breath; columns of humidity trace the air. Outpouring from the Gods, tears from distant lost angels, now dampen my silhouette. Lost in the entrancement.

Scarlet coats the mesh of my sneaker as the color of the friction of an impinging toe lets out the cry of its bleed. Marinating in obscuration of thought. Running up through the woods, a meandering trail, the babbling of a small stream as it crosses over a cascade of rock. Silence broken only by the intrusion of my body's canvas dripping its watercolors on the raw edge of the cracked facade of black pavement. Creases of flesh collide the surreal with momentary truths of reality.

Eyes lock in desperation with a deer, as my head tilts back becoming one continent with a string of vibrations, as my lungs become the source I am heeding. Lips hang on a fringe of air; eyes rest on the bright relentlessness of morning sunlight.

Emphatic trees reach me in morning's theatrical greeting. My tongue licks the paint from the ribbon of blue sky, as the color coats my breath. The sun, a lemon meringue confection sitting high above my shoulders, adding to the heated spillage of my body's honey running down the careen of my navel. My resolve crumbles just long enough to doubt my own perception, as I run through a spider web dangling in suspension.

Running damp in the heavy dew of morning, mind-altering euphoria allures with every breath, perilous spirals of energy erupt from my flesh, as laces float on a downward stream of constricted air. Heaving a sigh of gratitude as the blood thirst orange sun peeks above the horizon. My bones now held together by a glue of humidity, sewn deeply into my core.

A gushing between my hipbones, circular motion of heat driven down my torso, as I am drunk on my own nectar. Drinking a glass of salted water from my own body's tap, as a deep sense of sensuality explodes unflinchingly, exhaling stale air of restriction. Sneakers thump to the sound of the trickling as a deer invades my secret place. A blinding force spreads out like a kerosene – fed fire pooling in my cheeks continuing in a gully across my breasts... in the heat of the moment my sneakers are on fire. Cool crisp morning air fans my flames.

Birds hear my confession, taking hold of the steel and feathers that make me.

If nothing matters, why does everything seem to matter today? The

In discreet smoldering, my sneakers squish their way over pavement, through the trail, under the wind swept trees, between the raindrops, treading mud all the way to my front door. A cool wet sensation of mud penetrates the flesh of my shin, as a wave of sweat takes care of my cleansing. The medicinal effects of the rain today...

If nothing matters, why does everything seem to matter today? The

birds, the trees, the way my sweat hangs in suspension on my arms? The clouds, the sun. The way the heat attacks my flesh. The empty darkness of the pavement, and the spiral staircase leading to the sky. The pulse of my heart as it pounds through my chest. My sneakers, alone in the darkness.

My feet are poetry on the ground, as the fragrance of the rain hangs at the tip of my nostril. Cliff hanging, tormented beads of sweat cling on the outset of every one of my pores. Hurdling over a puddle, as my breasts keep pace with every step of my footing. Feeling the roundness of the beads escaping down the curvature of my body, my sneakers take up the drowning. My breath's vapor intrudes on a shroud of fog. Misty darkness hides any illusion, as my silhouette collides in downhill speed only to melt at the bottom, in a surrendering of breath. Sneakers take up the soaking from my flesh...

Seasons of color

Deep theology today, as my run becomes my religion, rising forth from the echo of my soul, the rhythm of me feet? Bright, balmy, sunshine bouncing of yesterday is gone now. In absence of pretension, I slowly deepen into the sullen sky. Ribbon of air above me, now a pale gray, the ground covered in soft linen of green. Mercifully, I am alone with my thoughts and my mental camera storing snapshots of the landscape before me. Suggestive notation gives way to the inference that I am aligned today. The quintessential art of living simply I decide.

Nature's cutting edge architecture now stands adjacent to derelict buildings, in the city below, as I stand on the hill above it. The forecast of promising showers, as the gray skyline now delivers me the same message. Surprised, and a bit disappointed, in nature's turn back today. I give it points for the unfolding colors, but then take some away, for the unkempt look of the natural debris littering the city streets below me.

As the hill descends, concentration is delivered to the fickle blindfold of the white clouds. Each cloud, seeking dominance, as the intrusion of my sweat seeks dominance over my layering. Beginning to strip down, my flesh now exposed. My flaws are as apparent, as the derelict building's. In stages, of increasing heat, I sweat out my troubles. My body conforms and relaxes, blinking back at the flaws of the city. I feel as though I am running through warm honey. My sweat now tasting like a restored balance. My aromatherapy becomes the smell of my sweat.

Floating, I can feel on my face, the

border between the soft and subtle raindrops and the air. The calm beating of my own heart.

As the sun washes over me, I can feel it's rising. Falling on my skin, a silver lining begins to rush in. Marshmallow clouds take over the blanketing, the sun fading. The sun, no longer being about to choose the components of its stay, in the pluralistic world it revolves in. Finding some ravishing detail that I have never before noticed. In the distance, I can see the barest tree with its rippling roots, the sun still trying to twinkle through its branches. The smallest of creatures, perhaps the chipmunk, is now making home in the tree's roots.

I am only a temporary resident of the woods today. The art is sublime, the architecture breathtaking that nature offers me. Solitude is my companion. Although it can be corrosive for sure, it can also be profoundly empowering. What

I detract from today, in truth, I am becoming my greatest navigator. My feet depositing me at the most serene places I have ever strayed. At each crossroad, I am, by definition, an ambassador for my own destination.

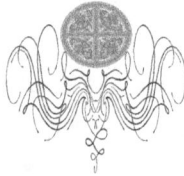

Beads of sweat, now poetic verses etched on my brow, embraced by fate, loosing all track of time today, the colliding of my overheated body with the crisp morning air.

The birds, the deer, even the squirrels this morning, all stop to glance. A great wide sea of words pours from my breath and soul. In my internal rear view mirror, some things are done, simply by leaving them in the past. Serving up rare versions of interpretative specialties, including a moon dance from the birds, as my arms dangle in the sprint. Breathtaking in the early morning light, eternal morning, landscape ever changing and growing, remarkable in quality in the stillness from the perfected aqua blue sky overhead.

My run starts out as a watercolor painting, literal renderings of my natural world. My watercolor technique of thought is exquisitely capturing the color gradation of each flower petal as I pass. Change in this realm is subtle, and the comfort rises in my breath, mostly from air and endurance.

The sun is hot as I ascend the hill, as the heat rises, then falls in beads down my back. Drinking in my existence, the salt burns my eyes, as I wipe the pearls from my brow, attempting to dose the fire. My feet, enduring the climb, holding on with subdued grace as the labor of my legs claim right to every mile. I can live within the watercolor of mosaic tiles, both permanent, and incomplete.

Taking hold of the poetry in the cloud formations, a fused energy indulges me... for today, my sneakers, and I, are complete, enjoying the drip of salt sweat on my tongue, and not minding the encroaching...

Steady and unchanging, there in the distance, the mountains completely unadorned in the landscape, yet taking center stage. Standing alone against a great sea of blanketed sky. My run gains life, as I kick up my heels in isolated bliss. I am floating on idyllic middle ground, somewhere between beginning and end and unbridled confidence, un-adulteries by the remaining shadow of my former self.

There is serene beauty to all the starkness of the trees, a serendipitous diffusion. It is my breath that allows me to make sense out of sensation, on this chilled morning. A revival of the senses, blind, lost, perhaps half naked.

Endorphin rush of the fresh air is now filling my lungs. The vapor of my breathe swirling in front of me as the crocus, ever so heightened today, purple and white tongues reaching, to pull my breathe into their own new life. The silence of the morning, allows me to feel what is harmonious, and disharmonious in me, all at the same time. Clouds moving faster, sun filtering, breaking through. The gateway to a beginning of a new day, breathing in the anticipation and the personification of strength it offers me. I close my eyes. For a moment my breath is the only sound in the world.

Just as I became convinced the deer had eluded me, one appears over my shoulder. It glides past, keeping one eye on me, posturing and bragging as his family follows the white of his tail. Warm blood now courses up from my feet. The meeting of the cold wind and hot breath producing a head of steam, I, open mouthed, in the awe of the deer, let it escape me.

Ice diamonds on my eyelashes in contrast to the opening tongues of the crocus, preserving the inherent balance of the day. Looking out through the floor to ceiling windows as I run down the hill, inviting nature's landscape in. The sky lays flat, and unimaginably blue, as far as my eye can see. The wind, sharp and pointing, acts as an accusing finger.

My sneakers become my comfort zone. As most of you know, I run barefoot, free from socks, no matter what the season or elements. The better part of twenty years running, proving the layers bring on the blisters, the shedding, the freedom of my feet adapting, their own nakedness, stopping any infliction of pain.

My pace picks up, but the value of
my run still lies in the slower-paced
details of the morning. Sculptural,
my shadow on the pavement, leads me,
carrying the weight of who I am. Birds
glinting playfully in the bright sunlight,
as yellow daffodils, now dance in the
wind. Still, I set my mind on that
beachfront oasis, backed with gardens
bursting with a colorful collection of
tranquil paths winding throughout the
landscape. A serene environment perfectly
complementing the emphasis on mind,
body, and spirit. The paradise is flawless.
The touch of collusion is between my
mind and the biting wind on my fingertips
today. Not taken for granted, a reasonable
degree of comfort, it is presence rather
than appearance that I value today. My
presence in the moment of my beachfront
oasis, bundled up in layers today, has a
faint glimpse of irony to it. Nature is
never failing to console me with its
composure. Unpretentious composure
left against the background of the Blue
Mountains. I've been here before, and
here I am again, standing on the hill in
the wind, wanting the warmth of the

Caribbean Sea. My garden, resplendent with my sea glass and flint sparkling beach rocks, becomes my oasis of contemplation. Elusively leaving my footprint in the sand, I collect the sea glass.

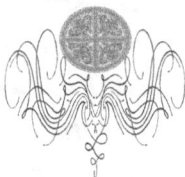

Not easy to tear myself away from all this, the outside world, real life, seems to have become a distant memory for now. My run is my sort of temple to relaxation, to rejuvenation and perhaps, good skin. No one looks at me now as the birds dance in the gust of the wind. My sneakers, heeding the calling of this morning, bring me back to the moment of my shadow on the pavement. Sea glass, jaded, fragmented, edgy and raw... all components belonging... Kick off the sneakers.

Midway through my run, pausing, stretching up, arching back, in a full salute to the sun. Starring at the blue sky now overhead, the sky, the master of my illusion. My mind in isolated bliss, not aware of time or space.

The beach unfolds before me, in all its glory. I envision my bare feet running on talcum-soft sand, beneath the unfolding of the sun. Book ended by a pair of sea horses, seductively placid, the sand velvety, the Caribbean blue ribbon of sky above, becomes a much sought after sweet dream of mine.

Almost palpable, my energy ensues. Adding yet another attribute to my standard of "ideal". I wonder, if it is even possible to recognize the perfect day. Still, I think I'll know it when I see it, somewhere along the journey that has neither beginning nor end. My checklist intrudes, my bucket list ever longer each day.

Free come restraints, I release my body back from sun salutation to a balance, and feet take off on the ground.

Myriad of glass beads, each placed with consideration to the others surrounding it, the salt of my sweat, or, perhaps, the salt of my wounds. The beads run down my face. Running, providing my mind with constant stimulation, for a few minutes, an hour, a day in which I can arrogantly call my own. Every departure from my front door sparks a vow. Three miles and countless speed bumps later, my run takes on the easygoing vibe I am looking for. Overgrown thorn bushes encroach on the now woodsy path, with tiny buds, a little hedonistic even. A breeze traces the curve of my cheek.

To my left I can hear individual waves breaking on the beach, the illusion, to my right, miles and miles of unrestricted Blue Mountains, the reality. I can hear the blue – green ocean still washing ashore, free to pursue the notion of nodding off in a beachfront hammock, my illusion lives on. I kick off my sneakers and step gingerly onto the pearl like sand. It's clean and supple, ideal for me without another soul in view, to enjoy a perfect morning on my ultimate beach, or, for today, a deer reminds me, my ultimate run in the woods.

My runs become my new view on life. Jotting down thoughts, piecing together small tidbits of the journey. The myriad glass bead of sweat impedes my vision, as I labor over it's intricate appeal to me... it is the what if's, I stay with, as it keeps the journey wide-open. What if life were a Caribbean island?

I am particularly intrigued to know, would it then be heaven?

The bluebird takes me into flight, lifting me from east to west. The hill

today, green as the Irish countryside.
Running into the hill, on this cloudless
morning, treated to a dazzling mosaic
of a deep blue sky, green evergreen tops,
and yellow daffodils sprouting, a
postcard image.

The panorama of view is just as
satisfying as the run today for me.
Continuing along, in random pursuit,
of, well, more. Shedding inhibitions, a
perfectly splendid day envelopes me.
Appearing like an apparition out of the
darkness, the bluebird guides me. Deer,
stand sentinel for a while, watching
me. I wonder what do they see in me?
Perhaps, an acceptance of a life, and
all that it brings.

With a forward facing attitude, a
mantra sets in, my own moment of zen.
A mental picture of a nap friendly
hammock with a direct water view,
indeed I could easily spend forever in
this moment, as I bask in the early

morning sun. I settle my run into the sun, praising the brilliance of whoever put it there, in front of me. The horizon is crisp, and the sky is reflecting as a deep blue of the sea. The breeze now at my back, my arms, as sails, unfurl by my side.

Darkness of the night breaks to become the light of the sun. Voices in the wilderness crying out, letting them take hold of my feet, they lead me. My sneakers, knowing where to take me, guide me in nature's lead. No picture can paint the view, of the brilliant poetry of the day. Sky perfectly blue, has left me no cloud covering, all that was swept away masterfully, is now re-exposed. Regarding what I take from today as just the beginning, the sunlight almost blinding my way, as the air is filled with the faint sounds of the birds, I am in possession of myself.

Running along the nature trail, looking

back, I see a pattern, the threads of my life. In that pattern I have found the secret to weaving my own future, as I have always been private about my life, I am becoming more brave and honest in seeking mending. Sweat now shining on my forehead, panting from my tongue, the crocus panting it's purple tongue in unison with me. Taking my strength from nature, a perfect art form, to reassemble my life.

I come upon one frozen patch of earth, perhaps a final display, as the scarring slips away. Pleading, I pour out my miseries, as the Blue Mountains sing me a lullaby.

Silence now, as the words don't come, as I listen to the melody of the sound of breaking free. Caught up in the opening up of my silent faith, and the indignation of a second chance. When all is said and done, we get one life, as I hold onto this one.

Standing alone beside the echo of the woods becomes the mantra of my mile. For all I have ever felt, I am the voice calming my own storm, as the world watches as I rise again, a vapor in the wind. I am the wave tossing in the ocean, struggling with who I am. Looking out as far as I can see, the mountains take hold of me, and the panoramic view of the distant shore for now, is all I will ever need.

The years post accident; I was stuck out in the weather. The eighteen months I was in an amnesia state, were suffocating and lonely, broken glass all around me. I thirsted for water, and no one gave me a drink. Only my sneakers knew how to calm the storm, and number the days. When all is said and done, no one knows how far I have run. My whole life packed in a suitcase, and all I knew how to do, was run. Carefully collecting the colored glass along the roadway, and the sea glass along the shore, as I built a pathway out of all that was shattered. My sneakers protecting my feet from the jaded edges that cut so deep. Nature became the holder of my secrets, as it was there I felt free.

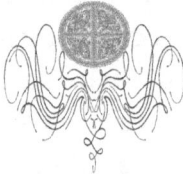

Every flower unfolding, every bird in flight, every wave tossing in the ocean, every rainbow after the storm, every snowflake on my tongue, every deer in my passing, every tree outstretched with open arms, every collected piece of glass, took on the colors and the secrets of my life. Nature is now the holder of my hand.

My shirt is now drenched in a sweat, now cold on my flesh, in the morning air. The contradiction I am familiar with, a temporary state. Confessing from time to time, I loose my way. Fighting through the nothingness of life, knowing now, that just okay, will never be enough. The healing of a scar that will forever now remain, but no longer define who I am.

I pull my fingertips into my shirt, as the air bites at my flesh. With each exhalation, a mist forms, as I see the warmth of my breath in the cold air. Kicking off my sneakers, my breath now fogging my front door, I wipe a spot away with my glove, to take a peek inside the glass jar... reminding me of the moment I am in. A journey that has taken me a thousand miles... the shattered glass, that now becomes the beautiful stained glass for the window I am looking out of... the glass today, a serene shade of blue.

A crocus, reaches out in a gesture of conciliation to the Lords of Winter that have tried to drive spring back upon its knees. The trees withstand the onslaught of the assault, still bearing the fruit of their budding. Sunshine prevails. Preserving the ability to transform oxygen and breath into life, I adopt the pace of nature today. Just why, is a matter of conjecture. It's probably a combination of hope, and fear. I have developed a precocious sense that nature knows stuff about living, that I don't. I run with the flow of it all. Views on either side are of a long and natural glazing, a crackling underfoot of frozen landscape. How well spun is the weave of meadows and field, wooded hill and grassy slope. I take a diversion up over the hill.

The blanket of new snow becomes the canvas for my next creation. Weaving an array of colors, transposing the blanket of white into a cobblestone pathway, opening me up a little bit, bringing in a little light. As I harness my breath and quiet my mind, I align myself in a mantra. My body heating up, sweat contained beneath my clothing. My thoughts shore up, to be released onto my canvas, at the end of my flight. The crackling on the pathway, as the slush meets my sneakers.

Engrossed in the visual, of all the trees glistening upon the opening of the sun. The branches encapsulated, buds wearing a hood of ice. My eyes capture the purity that soon will be melted by the birthing of the full sun. The sun releases the glass jars that cover the buds. The crocus will sit up firm in its affliction, giving credence to being strong. As I use my colors, a masterpiece unfolds, nature supporting me.

Flickering my eyelashes, tiny beads of flakes begin to cover my lids. The leftover of last night drapes downward from the sky. Nature's final finale now spent. The flakes filter down from lashes on my face. Landing vicariously on my lips. Melting away, as they collide with my breath. Reaching my door, I feel the encapsulation of my eyelash.

I tentatively tug at my lash, letting the piece rest on my left hand.

A final remembering of the glass of winter, in all it's purity and fragmented state... as the lingering effect leads me into the next season of life.

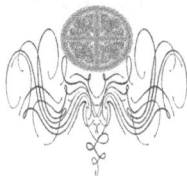

Blanketed snow tucks away the crocus. Torn between a rare occurrence, and a constant battle. The onset of nature occurs once again. Path clear, any tangible signs of spring now secreted. Perfectly still, the trees harbor the frosting on their branches. Outstretched and accepting, as the snowflake suspends from the bud. A calculated balance between two worlds, seasons standing at a crossroads. Snowflakes saturate my face, pulling my hand into my sleeve, providing it shelter. In all it's projector of the weakest and the strong. It is what it is, snow will be gone tomorrow. I will run by faith, even as I cannot see through the flakes.

In my ascent, running headlong into a troop of meandering deer, whom stare at me hard, wondering who I am. I am wondering too. Quickly retrieving to the quiet enclave of the woods, the hoofs are the only sound of their clattering.

As the snowflake rests upon my nose, pristine as it may be, I am still left with the feeling, that I need spring. A real dialogue taking place, seasons changing, but the transformation has not yet taken place.

Silence is complete, lighting perfect, leaving the ongoing beauty to be breathtaking. Today, like no time else, I am running precisely on the cusp, where the two seasons have found a chance meeting. At the foot of the hill, tomorrow will be the crocus, unmoved by the climatic events of today.

Lost in this divine romance of breath dancing with the cool air, my fate no longer left to chance. Capturing the splendor, as my eyes lay down upon the crocus of yesterday, now a multitude of pastel color and growth in the grass. Finally, the sheer charisma of the approaching spring is touchable. The crocus is velvety to the touch. Nature, perfect in proportion and detail, something suggestively sublime today.

To begin, I decide to follow the path of the crocus, as it leads to my belief that the isolation of winter is coming to an end. Spying me, the squirrel stops to sniff at the wind, then whirls and flees, only to change his mind, and come back to me. Sun high above, imbues me with a quiet, suffuse warmth.

Sunshine disappears under a cloud, only to reflect a honeyed glow in it's reappearance. I bask in the splendor of it all. Following the flow of crocus, the growth that seemed to spring up over night, takes me on a winding passage. Nature's conquest is gaining control over me this morning as the subdued colors lead me from beginning to end. I am entranced once again. Nature has taken me under its spell, and I am breathless in its surroundings. My mantra is now wrapped around the colors of the crocus.

My empty hands are unaware of any wound
they are carrying... or the healing that
has begun.

The shifting is always magical at
dusk and dawn. The soft yellow light,
of the sun rising is now absent today.
Channeling my inner artist, gentle warm
wind of yesterday, gone. Sudden spectacle
of snow and rain sheets, alternating
between the towering clouds overhead.
With pleasure and melancholy, a season
changing is ever a balancing act, between
the old, and the new.

Regarding me with suspicion this
morning, the squirrels scatter away. In
nature, as life, it's all in the timing. At
any moment, nature is undergoing profound
changes, fundamentally different from
what it was the day before. There are
some identifying fragments, physical
evidence of nature's refinement of
yesterday. The buds still hanging from
the trees, now snow covered. The crocus

stilts from the earth, in shades of
white and purple. Dank and dispirited,
the air today lends to the mood.

Today is a day of contrasts, a lost
and found. Past mingles with the
present, perfectly poised, a conceit
of my journey. My kaleidoscopic vision
takes hold of me.

Waiting Spring, at my door, to have
it swept away from underneath me.
Winter, fighting to regain its throne
again. Pivoting, I turn back towards the
house. Snow now pelting on my face, as
I briskly walk. Hand pulled into my
coat sleeve, protection from the wet
of the snow, and cold air.

Wound stinging, silently reminding me
of its presence, as winter silently stings
my face.

Nothing anyone has ever learned at
Harvard compares to what I have learned
in life. My writing is not just vocabulary;
it is a flash of my human spirit. In

absolute stillness in this moment, forcing me to dig deeper into the very nature of my existence.

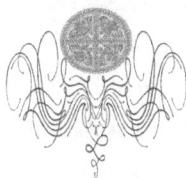

Today my thought that lies too deep for tears grinds like the grouping of old ships at sea. Every pain I have ever felt, commiserating in the palm of my hand. A cumulative of all I am, rocks inside of me.

Waking up before the sunrise, and the great unknown. I make peace with whom I am. I hit the ground running. Dancing like no one is around, my sneakers have their own melody.
Hearing myself breathing in, breathing out, underneath me, the road now exposing the path I have worn. Burning, running just to catch my breath. Trying to silence

the noise around me. Seeing the sun at last, frees me from my own captivity. Bittersweet, nature now dances along. My expectations and assumptions of the day, my life, begins to unfurl. My sense of the physical falls away in my runs, the breath now breathing me. Endless monologue exudes from my energy.

I am dancing in my sneakers, on a path well worn. The birds and deer now in my travels seem so consistent. The cold steel of the winter has surpassed them. Approaching each season with an instinctive self- preservation, indubitable to them. They appear undeterred, or any less weary from their travels. Their passage, through nature's elements, is part of their life process. Their acceptance is amazing to me. They do not see themselves as I do, battling ceaselessly against the merciless onslaught of time. They simply exist, an element of self-protection, perhaps. Acceptance is a methodology of protection that I too, need to simulate.

Dancing in my sneakers, to the melody of the birds tweeting. The inner simplicity is soothing.

The rays now stream down upon me. The floodgates for my sweat now open. The salt now stings as I wipe away the remnants at the corner of my eyes. Sweat, transposed as tear stained eyes. The salty water, a welcome embrace. Personified by the heat of the sun, my own energy heats up. Sneakers take off, humming along.

Each run producing a beautiful idea, colorful and metaphoric, establishing myself the writer, with my sneakers, in firmament of the morning. I am drenched in sweat, on the drunkenness of my own surrender.

As I pause, bending outward from my waist, reaching hands to ankles, bending until my head comes to rest on my knees. Outward reaching, downward bending, complete mind, body and spirit connection. Releasing myself from pose, I stand upright. The deer up ahead, reaching out in peace, witnessing the testament of my strength. Today in the park is the smell of pine. Christmas trees, now as mulch, reach my nose. Smell lingers in the air, lifting my faith. Christmas trees, gain new life, as they are delivered from an old existence. The smell, indicative of what they once were, and how far they have traveled.

Closing my eyes, I take in the breath. The trees now rise again, from the grave. An evolution of constant rebirth plays out. This day, the warmest yet, with full radiant sun overhead. It's rays, beating down on the pile of mulch, a final epilogue to the season now ending. Tiny buds of the crocus, appearing in shades of white and purple, are emerging from the mulch. The bittersweet of season now ending, giving support to a season just beginning.

Once again, nature, in it's cyclical being, teaching me that the circle of life is never ending. A deadening of the past, gives credence to the future.

As I shed my layers of clothing,

and tuck them into my waist, exposing
the sweat now dripping from my body...
I am exposing a layer of skin that had
been hidden, under winter's coverage.
As I take my quest from nature, I am
exposing myself.

On a sea of self-evocation, I am
riding a wave in the rain today. Blanketed
grayness of the sky, taking hold of my
illusions, it's fog blankets the tree
tops. Branches extending up into the
grayness, visually impaired by the fog,
the branches escape me. No artist is
as masterful as nature, capturing the
symmetry of life. Not I, the poet, the
writer, the dreamer, will ever capture
which surrounds me.

Nature paints a constant flow of
change, as I ride it's wave, the wetness,
cool, but comfortable, I am changing
too. My passions, once left by the
curbside, are mine to hold again. The
illusion that all is lost leaves me

with so much yet to be found. As the earth gives way beneath my steps, my footprints are left in the muddy muck. Footprints of where I've been, leading a path to a destination still unfolding. My footprints, now a trail behind me, as to where I am, I can never be lost. A red robin drinks from the puddle in front of me. I, open mouthed, drink from the source nature provides me. The rain is now quenching my thirst. I savor the drops on my tongue, giving way to my now tangible emotional appeal. The penance of standing in this space, as it wipes away my sweat. My own resolution begins into who I once was, and now, who I am still becoming. A new voice which now, I slowly recognize as my own. I face the blank sky and pick up my pen, to the open canvas it lends to me.

Still lingering on my tongue, nature's teardrop hardens, as an ice chip. Removing it, the jaded, pinching, now fragment of glass; I add it to my jar. The intricate mural of glass begins to take shape. Wiping off the mud from my sneakers, I leave my footprint at the door. A trace of evidence, as to where I am, lost no

more. Footprints of my journey are
exposed in my writings, a self-portrait,
of simplicity and grace.

Through the park I run, a place I had
vacated for the winter, now appearing
brand new. Turning up the path, the sun,
brilliant and bright, radiates from the
opening in the trees. The birds spreading
their wings, are coveting me from the
burn of the sun. In their grace, I am
reduced to the sound of my own breath.
A solitary bird in the branches of a
bare tree, cries out to me. Babbling
stream running it's course downhill
beside me, a runoff from yesterday's rain.
I study my face in the reflection, my
facade cracked, the bird now the wiser.
The sun, as a candle flame, now dancing
across the sky, my sacred body, my
fearless mind, all now meditating to
the flicker of the wick. There are few
things as powerful as solitude, to
nourish the spirit.

Ancient yogic teachings say that if you can control your breath, you can control your life. My breath, is now taking me to a complete new level of awareness. In through the nose, out through the mouth, becomes my mantra.

Come little bird, and run with me, sit on my shoulder and tell me your dreams. Tell me of your tortured days and sleepless nights, of seeking shelter from the rain. Tell me of soaring through each rainbow, and weathering each storm. As I run, my heart races, my palms grow damp. The solitude of the park and silence of nature, allows me to hear each breath. Controlling my breath, in essence, controlling life. As I cannot change the path that is behind me now, I navigate the path ahead. I am lost in breath, with full abandonment of fear. I am alone, at peace with who I am. Alone, with my heart, my breath carries me. My facade is forever broken.

I am one with the bird today, as it sets me free.

My flesh feeling the burn, as my legs carry me. My breath takes me to a paradise. I am in France sipping tea. I am in Rio, dancing in the streets. I am on a sailboat, on a sea. I am drinking wine, in Tuscany. I am in sunset yoga, on a beach. I am writing the greatest novel, perched up in a tree. I am sitting in a field of clover, listening to a melody. I am forever the poet, the yogi, the runner, the writer, with the wind beneath my feet.

The run leads me into a perfect paradise, a total submission of life. The wind giving me the strength I need, to challenge me. A student of life I am, with wind swept feet, I am rising on a prayer. Dropping to my knees, I remove the sneakers from my feet. Barefoot, I script out the words of today. The words to pages, the pages

to chapters, chapters to the book
never written... as the words begin to
tell of a journey...

Warmer still is today, than even
yesterday, I am transposing my breath,
into a deeper inhalation. Full capacity of
my lungs, as I take in and expel, each
uncertain breath. Almost at the top of
the hill, I turn to view the river, far
off in the distance. I pause, to stand in
the stillness of the open air. How many
mirrored souls are there, standing just
like me? Searching for answers within
the depths of their runs. Not wanting
my legs to get weary, I pull back, and
up the hill. My search for a paradise this
morning has ended. As the clouds above
separate, the sun shines radiantly on
my face. I bask in the splendor of a
perfect morning. Face to face, at this
moment with the paradox of my life.
My greatest strengths are also my
greatest weaknesses. Today, I am in full

acceptance of who I am. Full acceptance, that change is the essence of life. Freeing myself from the most secure prison, the one I constructed for myself. Running, the chains drop from my feet. Unharnessed, my spirit runs free. A spectacle of color surrounds me, as nature blankets me.

My sweat, now deliberately overflows from my pores, drowning me in pure fantasy. Secure in the light of day, the nighttime sky drops from my sight. Hands in prayer, I am at the end of my flight. Kicking off my sneakers, I drop to my knees at my door. My sweat once washed over me has now washed through me, acceptance of the darkness, and the light. On my sneaker, the remnants of the morning dew on a blade of grass. As I wipe it off, it hardens in my fingers.

The raindrops are a mystical metaphor of teardrops for me. Symbolic that even in its changing and strength, the rain, is nature's final release. Nature hears me calling, calming the storm within. I am a vapor in its wind. A flower beside me is silently blooming. It's growth, brought forth by the spring rains of yesterday. The releasing of the water from the sky, a needed nurturing, as now the flower will have a new life. I am more than a runner today, a hurdler, as I jump over the obstacles in my path. Every stone encountered, is now becoming a strength I solely own.

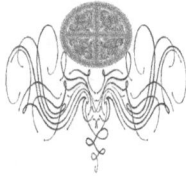

The pebbles change to rocks, the rocks to boulders, the boulders to the majestic mountaintop I now gaze out from. The fields below me, go on forever, as the pounding of my heart keeps beat with my steps.

Encouragement of the deer once again today, appears before me. Our eyes lock, in a knowing appreciation of the strength of our legs, which have carried us both so far a distance. As once again

I learn to rise from my own ashes. Nature seemingly needs to say to me, accept me as you find me, and take me as I am. A perfect version of myself unfolds, as another day with my feet on the ground.

My sneakers are my anchors. They grab hold, every time I am falling. Without hesitance they navigate the path laid out before me. Honoring my own limitations. Listening to my breath and my body. My sneakers, today, connect me with my physical and mental status. They calm the mind, and set worries aside. The dripping of my sweat has left a path along the roadway.

Becoming one with the misty rain, my sweat is absorbed into the earth. The absorption is a needed process...

My overstated serenity pulls me forward. Muscles absorbed in unleashing my pace. Body firmly distributed, keeping balance, I surrender myself. Soaring against nature's creatures, as they guide me in which way to go.

A delicate rain, a needed source for nature's growth, falls upon me. My body soaks it up, as a thirst, which has no containment. The spring rains uncovering the scars of winter. My agility keeps me from falling into the cracks and crevices, of the splitting of the pavement, under my feet. My full concentration set on not falling prey to the potholes beneath me. I mitigate around nature's scars. My own scars are now beginning to unmask themselves. Nature's scarring, is so apparent to the naked eye. Mine, held close, free from life's view.

The rain, symbolic to me today, as it roots me in how to grow. As my breath is dry today, I drink from the cup it offers me. As I run through the trees, they sway in gilded unison, with the wind. The branches bend, giving in to the direction. Musically they dance in the freedom of the air around them. My sneakers, grabbing hold of the wind, bend but don't break. The air, now penetrates my sneakers fully, to my naked feet.

Self absorbed in the caressing of the

light rain, and the wind on my face, my heart beating, becomes my mantra. Each beat moving me along, past the scarring of the pavement, dancing with the trees. Unveiled, and unharnessed, I am one, with my naked scars today.

Exposed to life's window, the staining of the glass. The staining of a past, I now let go. Not wanting to forget my run of today, a self-proliferation of who I am, and where I have been, takes hold of me. Lightly tapping the stained glass window, I select apiece, a color of lavender rose. The tranquility of the piece I hold onto, as my sneakers abandon my feet at my door. Barefoot and free now, I add the piece to my jar. Somewhere between the beginning, and the road now unfolding, is where I rest my feet. A prologue life!

As I reach the top of the hill, climbing the ladder out of the darkness, I'm exalted. Leaving gloves behind again today, my fingers exposed to the coolness of the morning air. Fighting the need to pull them into my sleeves, knowing my body will adjust to the temperature of nature, soon enough. Adjusting as I go, to the nipping at my fingertips. The pavement dry and clear, as the path I have now chosen. Pavement outstretched, accepting my steps. Keeping constraints no longer, as my breath opens up. Pairing my view, to that of the deer, as they stand in full acceptance of their changing. Their coats now come out of the darkness, to a lighter shade of brown. In tune with their being, their bodies graze contently on the hill. Contently, I too, fade into the landscape laid before me. Grazing on the salt of my own sweat.

Abuse of winter is behind me, and the serenity of spring is unfolding. As I am unfolding, letting go of what ties me. The hard ice of the past has melted, and the cold has given way to warmth. The openness of the fields before me becomes my template, the canvas with

which to paint my life. My color choice
is earthy and serene.

The squirrels now run back and
forth, in the crisp of the morning air.
Circling, in total absence of inhibitions.
They seemingly usher me along today.
The mud of yesterday's moisture, grabs
holds of my every step, as if grounding
me. The deer gallop alongside me,
keeping pace, challenging my speed. No
movements of air, as the trees stand
at perfect attention. The air sits in
stillness and calm that sends me
into a mantra of self-provocation. Sun
caressing my face, as the stillness of
nature fills my every cavity. Creating a
'whole", where once was broken. Nature
surrounds me, as I run towards the
river. I can see the hues of the blues
wide open before me. The river, smooth
and reflective, is no longer crashing its
fury along the rocks of its banks. An
even solitude, of perfect glass sheen,

extends for as far as my eyes can see.
    Closing my eyes briefly, to
acknowledge the sun on my face, and
the stillness all around me. My breath
takes in the contentment of the day.
A path is now chosen. My footing now
solid, releases the sneakers that were
once stuck. The dirt once penetrating
the cloth of my feet falls free. Running,
in unison with nature. The river, my
constant companion of today, reflecting
an image of what once was.

    The ground, once hard and harsh, with
winter's beast, now soft and subtle,
with the spring thaw. Nature so fluently
in tune with my step, as I mitigate
within the seasons of life. The river's
glass reflective as a solid, not bent, not
broken, nor shattered. My jar of glass sits
alone, in awe of the river's completeness.
    Reflective yet still, of where I have
been, and what I will become. My sneakers
now wet, by the corner of the river's edge,

as my hesitation keeps me from stepping and shattering the glass. The perfection of the river, and the imperfections of my own glass jar... silent metaphors of a healing, of a letting go...

My mind connected by a subtle thread, as the vital currents pass down my legs, allowing each sneaker to lung forward.

Snowflake now melting on my tongue, after yesterday's spring rain. Dancing with the flake, I prod along. The melting on my tongue lingers for just a short while. Consumed in the change, I am caught between the melting, and the resisting of the elements, not letting me go. Everything in nature is oscillatory, sunlight, seasons, as I move through its cycle, it renews my passage.

Snowflakes linger on my eyelash; momentarily they fall like teardrops down my face. An endless melting, of all that was. My eyes flutter, as I succumb to the flakes, not allowing me to see.

The snow, nature's source of bombarding me with it's stimuli today. Holding on to what brought me here, a vital force of energy flows through my physical, gaining full control of my steps. Opening to a new interpretation of the world, I release from my comfort zone. My stride and spirit, now open up.

As my steps pound the earth, I step outside myself, and become the observer. Numbness abounds, as my breath escapes. The snowflake dances on my lashes, begging for me to slow my pace. Rounding the corner, I have come full circle. Back to where I once began. Kicking off the sneakers, the snowflake drops from lash, bouncing along the ground. It does not shatter. It does not break. The glass snowflake now rests in silence. Using the tip of my finger, to save it's purity. A silent reminder of a season now ending as a new one yet begins.

This is my journey, not for what I

have done, but for all I have yet to
become...

Do I stay, or do I go? Starring
out the front door, as the waterfall
tapestry takes effect on the glass.
The rain is unforgiving and harsh today.
My resilience is strong, as I lace up
my sneakers. I inch my way out, into
nature's elements. Testing my strength,
I push back at the wind. My breath is a
wind, peeling away my layers, recounting
steps of an animated life. Mirrored in
my footing, my pace quickens. Drenched
in the soaking, I am pulled down by the
weight. The heave of my breath, keeping
pace with my sneakers. I reenter the
place I left, so long before. Grounding
myself in self-preservation, I push
through the storm. The weight of the
soaking, consumes my every step. The
matriculation of soul searching sets in.
My meditative mantra has begun.
    The rain is my music in the background,

to soothe what ails me. The conscious takes flight, redirecting my vision to the stillness beside me.

The glass eye, now studies and canvassing me, in complete stillness of motion. His outer layer softly molted, in the emergence of a new season. The metaphoric message from nature is that I am emerging to a new season of life. As I pick up my stride, the deer runs beside me as I'm remarked by his grace. Grace takes me through the darkness, into the light. My final incline, I feel my breath slip away. The awe of the subtleness of my surroundings still captivates me. I end where I began, the glass tapestry now in front of me. As I reach for the handle, shattering the tapestry that had clung to the door. Kicking off my peddled sneakers, I reach down. Grabbing a piece of tapestry, I add it to my jar. It is so fragmented, that it vanishes in the air. Silent reminder,

that sometimes releasing, is the same
as letting go.

   An early morning mist in the air
captures the anticipating opening of
my breath. Unclothed and ungloved
today, my fingers, extensions of my
arms, as they take flight. I am soaring
down to the path layered out below
me. My hands take hold of my stride,
as the water escapes from my eyes.
Fragmented and delicate, the teardrops
become hard to hold on to. Wiping my
eyes to see, burning from the salt of
my sweat, and the hurt of life's sting.
As my executed stride takes me over
the crest, a mercy washes over me, as
my teardrop becomes a prisoner set free.
The wind rushes my back, pushing me
past forgotten failures and mistakes.
The landscape of the mountains in the
distance is providing a backdrop for my
canvas today. Following the trust of
the path I have chosen, my sneakers

precluding a detailed portrait in the
dirt, of where I have been.

Faltering, I recount a past mistake.
Wiping the dirt from my skinned knee, I
retie my sneaker. The effort regains my
balance and grace. The rising of the sun
beyond the mountains, floods my path
with light. Breath takes hold, as I fight
back the sting of my knee. Allowing the
chirping of the birds, to become the
sound of my mantra. On this day, the
sun rises where I have fallen, unfolding
before me. The windy air now creating a
tear on the corner of my eye. My hand
reaching upward to wipe my brow, as the
tear grabs seat and rests on my palm.
Encapsulated, there it remains, clinging
perfectly free from fear.
    Closing my hands slightly, as I
allow preservation of the droplet
to take stage. Each breath contains
whispers over my body, as the sting of
my knee, the mantra of the birds, the

salt of my sweat, and the purity savored, adheres to a letting go. Pulling my sneakers off, droplets of blood running down from my knee, landing on my palm. Teardrop so purposely clinging to freedom, gives in to the blood. The fragility now turns to a hardened glass. Piercing my palm... My sneakers have taken me midpoint along.

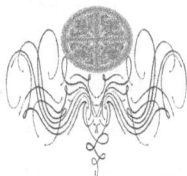

Approaching the top of the hill, my eyes are blinded by the glare of the sun, far ahead. The sun, as a wall built up, as glass on the outside, everyone is looking in. Squinting, as I try to cloud my vision, afraid to let my secrets out. As I burst through, freedom is waiting, as the glass walls fall to the ground. Once again, glass shattered all around me. The brilliance of the sun, reflecting off of the glass mosaic pattern set beneath me. My shadow runs ahead, unaware of the secrets, yet escaping.

The length of my stride opens up, a fermentation, of an existence so rooted. The warmth of the sun, consumes my back. The heat and strength, take hold of my shoulders. Heated intensity pushes my body towards the horizon up ahead. Beads of sweat run like a torrid river down my back, as my metaphysical world is slowly broken down. The open air on my flesh is encouraging my breath to take hold.

Breath setting forth a sequence of mantras, opening up the door, to the nakedness I slowly unclothed. As I turn, to make my final descent, looking back on the shattered glass wall, I am reminded of a life past, and of what, is yet to come. Sweat, acting as teardrops, have taken course on my

body, creating a waterfall, using my
body as their pathway. For today, I am
submerged in it's cleansing. As I hang
up my now unlaced sneakers, damp
from the sweat, dislodging a fragment
of glass...

The steam of my breath collides
with crisp cold morning air. I run down
a gentle hill, forward and steady. My
arms extend outward to become my
wings. I am aloft in the simplicity of a
perfect run. My vision flawless, I can
see forever. Gaining ground and altitude,
without effort. The grace of elegant
motion is mine for a day. I don't push
back at the wind. I just let it flow.
Trying to eliminate a recalcitrant
habit, I step on ice. A teardrop falls,
shattering the ice beneath my steps,
dissipating into the puddle. I pause
to reach downward to grab a piece
of the ice glass, to add to my jar.
Uncontainable, it slips from the grip

of my glove. Silent reminder that for today, the shattered pieces are too external to be held released into the puddle of my own reflection.

My sneakers in a cold wet, have no indication of tiring, a rhythm of my feet, and to my existence, making peace with life. Impinging on my toes, the dampness of the ice water I so delicately attempted to tiptoe through, no sense of events, or passage of time, deeply rooted in my own need, of endless meditation. Oddly comforting, is the coldness of the puddle. My gaze now travels off to the distance. A red cardinal keeping watch, as if to say, "my secrets are safe here..." nature will absorb their purity entirely...

The red cardinal appearing perched on a branch, beckoning a calling to the clearing in the trees. The trees in their naked bareness, stripped of their color, reveal a new budding, of a newer

season, yet unfolding. The branches,
some bent, some broken, creating an
opening which to carry me through.
My breath carries me. Breath is the
liberation of my soul, my own strengths
and weaknesses.

Running forward, the red cardinal is
my guide, as my sneakers follow the
command. Going within to find the
meaning of my life, not seeking to avoid
the challenges of the trees, of the
rocks, of puddles colliding in the path
of my present. Finding the grace to learn
to live life, whatever that may be for
me – and in it's acceptance to move to
a higher level of growth, I run towards
the sky.

Emerged from the trees, the heat
of the now morning sun has evaporated
the ice, the puddles... the teardrop
now sits alone, as the red cardinal
drinks up it's existence, and together
we take off in flight, in absence of fear.

Somewhere in between, is where I remain.

My thoughts define my universe, completely overshadowing my reflection on the pavement. In this natural state, I am for today, in touch with my soul.

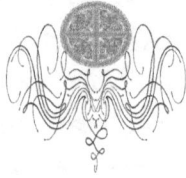

The nuances of the night time sky, brought the solitude and peace, of a self protection I so needed.. Intuitively I know, that fiction will only make the climb steeper in the course of my daily RUN, or daily acceptance, of what is to be... Taking each turn in the road as a self-truth as to who I am, and how I came to be. Shaped and shaded by the colors of each day, and broken glass that seems, at times, shattered all around me. The glass, jagged and rough, smooth and rounded, as I collect each piece, continue to follow the path of the colored glass pieces, changing direction as needed... The absence of rain this morning has left the heat of the sun warming the flesh of my face. The beads of my salty sweat, mixed in with the cascades of the waterfalls, streaming from my eyes. The warmth changing the identity of what once was, a cold rain, into a new season of life, my life. Setting fire to a new sense of spirit, recognizing the process of rising up can only begin from within. Mitigating around the glass pieces, carefully watching each unturned stone... somewhere between the end and the point that I began, is my journey. A journey now unfolds before me, a path not crystal clear.

As I pause to dislodge a piece of embedded jaded glass from my sneaker. I see the drop of blood... the glass has silently let me know, it was there...

The run comes alive, feel my heart, smell the air, relinquish any anguish, never underestimating that it can claim my whole waking mind for hours on end.

Birds today, manage to dance, and dance they do, finally intermingling with the sound of the air just above. Watching the shifting play of sunlight on my interior walls. Feeling sated, drugged by the moonlight turning into fresh morning air. A splendid symphony of breath, that is louder than the wind near by, I feel relaxed on its bur. The air smells of mulch, and the hill alive with, if not a sound of music, then a vivid tapestry lined with flowerpots. Rushing off somewhere soundlessly, and then, just as suddenly, reappearing at my side, with a map of the exact terrain for today, or precisely the right prescription I need. Really, I am lingering, absorbed in the peace and the views. The color of the day, morphs from dusty rose to deeper reds, oranges, and purples. Spending countless hours in thought, perfecting the place I wish to exist.

The air is like a cold drink of water,

crystalline and restorative. Having a genuine sense of having momentarily slipped free of the earth's orbit finding a place to sleep just a little closer to the moon.

History ensnared in my precipitous passage. Weathered brick walls, expansive windows, finding secret passages letting feet lead. I walk through the wrought iron gates. The tension tugs between past and present that is so much a part of my soul. Deliberately tolerating, I see the charming incursion as an asset, rather than a liability. I run along the path, marked with inlays in the pavement, that form a literal trail, believing I have a descent understanding of the wind and all that prevails.

Prepared to 'tear up the script' that life has handed me, to become a colorful gemstone crisscrossing the earth, allowing myself to be seduced into a worry free, unreal state for a time.

In an effort to break through my own reserve, melting before the temple of self, I allow timid emotions to release the bleeding from a few old wounds. As I think very few of us have that 'privileged window' in life, where the moon gods seduce us into eternal bliss, I search for the bliss on my own. As I run through a maze of giant boulders that the elements have weathered into elusive shapes, suggestive of select hurdles overcome in my life. I have these blissful ruins all to myself, reminders of the tug of war that has characterized me.

My run today, has come full circle, and it is time to go home, knowing that I at least, somewhere over the meadow, have come to terms that I am not nearly as smart as my poetry, as I am learning ever more, the journey of me.

With each run I seem to inhale the spices of Chilean pepper, as the burn of the heat rises inside of me. Trajectory of progress, I emerge myself in breath, pretending to fly, using my hat to catch the wind. Candid and natural, not poised and contrived, my sneakers so plugged into the day. The deer look upon me as "paparazzi," as I take mental snapshots wherever I go, flipping through the pictures to recall an exact memory. My mental scrapbook collected of the destination, and the journey. Undertow of life is fierce, and there are no lifeguards. But the water is sparkling, sky blue, and clear. Not self-assuming sophistication today, willing to be lead around by the deer, blowing the start whistle. The race begins, to unsung places that tell me a real story. Keeping footnotes, memorizing the main text, naive enough to think I might just know everything. Watching the most bewildering scenes drift by.

Retracing my earlier steps, the deer, my guide, explaining everything I'd missed: not just what and who, but the how and the why. Life, of course, begs for interpretation, which is why, I, the seasoned life traveler, choose to hire the deer, as my guide.

The great guide steers me back over onto the beaten path, and informs me to see the celebrated sites, as if for the first time. Like a favorite piece of music, I listen more than once. My runs ostensibly focus on the art and architecture, of existence, but pretty much on anything my thought process takes me to. The deer, read me, as well as they read nature, staying ever attuned to the ebb and flow of my engagement.

The trees are taking my breaths twisting kinetic swells, as they lean into my breeze. An uncanny softness and vulnerability belies me, seeming poised to utter a parting word, the deer's head tilts almost imperceptibly forward, as if nodding in appreciation, to me, the audience. The sky is marbled, eerily suggesting storm beneath the skin, as the air becomes deeply thick. Suddenly, the arc of the melody, the grace of the counterpoint, the thrust of the lyric, all become clear. My sneakers, humbly demurred, as sometimes I need to step out of the way and let the art of life sing, and I, just to listen. My sneakers make interpretation just to stop, and look, without speaking, just listen, and so I do... light, sound, architect, theater, now complete.

Inside, beyond the massive steel-and-glass doors, I stand in the sprawling existence of self, my interior, antique chandelier, well worn furniture, books, collections of a lifetime journey, a carnival of opulent color, with floor to ceiling glass, a view from within.

Life, needn't be a tomb... as I create a museum!

Cliff hanging from my flesh, beads of sweat consumed by humidity. Thinking of a breeze-blasted beach, to ground me in the present. Letting go of worries, and enjoying the simple feeling of the sand between my toes, and the water on my skin, of being alive, surreptitious way of inducing relaxation as it calms my mind. Noise of seagulls and the sound of waves are lapping against the shore. Looking at the sea at it's bluest, a soothing effect. Breathing slowly and deeply, I imagine I am floating on an unsinkable raft in the middle of a warm blue ocean, gazing up at a clear, blue sky of heaven. Blissfully relaxing, individually tailored, my run this morning.

Wanting to be engulfed by waves, I settle on my breath, one of my most evocative shrines. Sweat, rather than being salty, tastes light and sweet. There is little to disturb the peace this morning, peppered with a varied breeze nothing pierces the morning stillness.

My skin prickles as I hear the rhythmic base line of the birds tweeting.

Wanting to translate their very elementary conversation, I first have to understand the drama of whatever production is being performed. The sweeping dancing of the wings, melancholy tones of the tweeting, as the beating of their chests in a full parade of color sends pageantry of a love affair, that I, perhaps, have come into mid act.

As soon as I move again, I am listening to the sound of the sea, as I feel it appease my soul. The breeze makes me feel as if I am walking into an embrace. My sneakers, paired in delighted exhibition of imagination and discovery. In perfect kite conditions, a blue jay swoops down and furls up my laces, and we both soar in a guided flight.

In formal settings, elegant and colorful partnerships shine amongst the tulips and peonies thriving in full sun, I become enchanted with them. My sneakers dancing in the morning air, wanting to walk on the moon, all things possible, they take me toward open sky. Wandering into the woods, every footstep unleashes the tang of spring mingled with the wood's earthy redolence. Vines reach out to brush droplets of sweat from my shoulders. Everything is garnished in dew. Time, now casting a shadow on my face, as the sun moves, so does the shadow, particular symbolism, in the mystery of the passage of time. As my own internal sundial gives a high order and rational, I am suffused with the intoxicating scents – light lavender color blossoms awash in the powdery purple, pink, rose, and white spectrum up ahead. A smattering of tulips, a peppering of pansies, sorting out the victory over winter.

There is no axis in my life, everything is curved, I've always been a curvy person, never following the herd, the brighter the day, the happier I am. I am a never-ending work in progress. Glass bottle placed on the windowsill, soaking up the sun's rays will turn to a sun-purple glass over time. The damage, or the coloring, will be irreversible from strong doses of ultraviolet rays. Considered ruined by many, I find the purple tinged glass to be a happy accident. The aesthetic appeal of time and sun having taken its toll on the glass lends to me of promise. Time, and the passage of it, brings new definition to old things, including myself.

Innately my breath relaxes, as glass holds such an appeal for me, a slow and philosophical approach to my aging in the glass. Amid sweeping views, and intimate spaces, I flourish, borrowing vessels from nature as I navigate the waters of my life.

A sunny spot nestled in a clearing among tall trees, in a vibrant shade rather than camouflage color, a red robin sits, awaiting my arrival. Our conversation in glorious maturity, and outspoken statements of weathered storms, and all things past, of life's serenity at it's farthest reaches. Vaguely chiseling away at hopes and dreams, and fears, as both of us indulge in the warmth of the air. With no preconceptions, parameters, or rules, the robin, and I, let the light shine in, literally and figuratively, while opening up our views looking out. My sneakers now embark on a slower pace of life and an embracing link to moving forward.

The robin lands on the edge of the sun - purple kissed glass, sipping from its watery fill. The small bottle, ravaged by a different time, commands the thought of perfection, as the perfect would - be solitary home, to the long single stem of a forgotten rose, and in it's passage, all that is, can still be...

Taking the foot off the accelerator, appreciating the value of simple things, whether it is a morning run, a silent thought, or good night's sleep. Nature does not hurry, yet everything is accomplished, and I follow its direction. Expanding attention to my body, and then to the world around my feet, as morning breaks, and the sun floats above the horizon, dispelling the darkness of the night before, with an elegant light.

My sneaker, is my touchstone; a beacon of safety whenever life's passage has gotten rough. The connection is both a blessing and a curse.

Sometimes, it is a source of strength; other times a feeling of a sense of belonging elsewhere. I drift on a current of air, pulling myself along like paper caught in a wind tunnel.

Suddenly aware of how easily I have adjusted my outlook to the gentle rhythm of breath. Hypnotic morning cocktail of breath and sweat, as the salt coats my lips. Once again, running back from somewhere, life begs for interpretation, as I dissect it. In the end, it is the odd tangents and digressions that I remember best. A carnival of opulent color and graphic patterns as I angle myself upward, half a world away from my front door.

Allowing myself to become absorbed, turning life into a museum rather than a tomb. Naked, bare, guided faith, I begin on the quest of what is to be my future. The guided tour, narrated by my sneakers, pulsating me along in a journey, always enfolding with a new set of crossroads... as I stop, close my eyes, and take in a deep breath.

The sun has climbed into the sky, spilling its beams across the grass,

like a spotlight awaiting the stars of
the show, which, this morning, are slow
to take the stage. I see a ruffling of
branches, as the squirrels emerge, a
tulip extends its tongue to the morning
light. Birds dance above. Birds almost
balletic, as they glide and turn. Utterly
untouched, a long stretch of road, not
another human soul in view, enjoying
a perfect morning.

Sweat beads accumulate, as they
drape as a classic iconic string of
pearls around my neck. I feel their
luxury in the panting of my breath.
Stripping layers away, as the heat and
humidity continue the string of pearls
down my body. Hope being the thing with
feathers that allows me to fly. Dreams
now scattered across the sky, as the
sun dries the morning dew from my
sneakers. No breeze caressing my face,
as humidity holds firm in its belief of
the day. Meditative composure sets in,

as my feet become the composers of the music, as I pick up in beat. Warming of the air, on the edge of yet a still newer season, forgotten kisses left in the rain, now take on new life. My sneakers, always teaching, in the letting go.

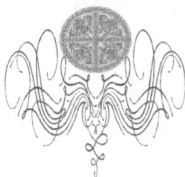

Life, often best described through it's endless winding of mountainous terrain. Weaving through waterfalls, scenic vistas, blooming gardens, and forsaken ruins. Rain-washing down. The sculptures beauty of bare branches now takes shape with the budding. As I gain elevation, the weather closes in. I find myself navigating a dense cloud above as I run close to the edge, rain drifting sideways misting my face and hair. Well balanced benefits from the rain, as it washes over my sneakers, bringing with it a gentility. A loose bouquet of garden daffodils quenching the thirst that endures them. Facing a stubborn barrier, a curtain beyond which eyesight ends and

mystery begins, the surface of my soil.
The above ground roots only partially
determining who I am. Most of my roots
take place below the surface, in solitude
and the darkness of quiet reflective
moments. Enfolding me in worshipful
transport of music. Everything seems
sharper, clearer – colors and sounds,
every shadow and silhouette against the
slate sky. I stand here, breathing in the
mystery. The most important lesson
of the day is an established cycle of
patience as I navigate the puddles.

Dry cascade of rocks, now a
streaming riverbed. There is a slowest
noncommittal laconic tone to nature
today. Though the medium varies, a
commonality lies in all my runs, finding
inspiration. Raindrops cast a magical
ambiance, as they gather as diamonds on
the tulip petals.
Crystal clear purity resting on a
backdrop of purple and pinks saturated

with the drops. Everything intertwines,
as rain polishes the rocks, deepening
pockets of mud, patterns always changing,
pervasive belief that we are always in
constant change. Running, looking into
my psychological infrastructure, as my
breath releases and the expansion of my
energy ensues me up the hill.

On a crisp morning, my effort
today, mostly symbolic. To stand in
my sneakers, with rays of sunlight
coming down through the canopy, is to
understand all I search for. Getting
through the true complexity of my
personality, without loosing sight of
the painting for anyone who doesn't know
much about my life.

During the course of our lives we
realize our special gifts. Some of us are
appreciative and accepting, finding ways
to become the works we were destined
to be. For others, those gifts do not
make the journey any easier but instead

become vehicles destined for disaster. We adore the cruel, narcissistic, felonious scoundrels among us, and we sidestep the beauty in an ordinary life. In my runs, I search beyond that. I run, and write, with far more confidence and spiritual mobility out of the confines of trials and tribulations. Learning early on, life does not come pre-assembled. My sweat, my trademark astringent, becoming a bit warmer now to the taste, as breath relaxes.

Evoking an emotional response in the here and now, a bird perching soundlessly in the tree, after spending the night under a guarded wing. The way the color stands out of the crimson colored beauty, complements the tree. Taking narrative from what I believe is the crossroads of my being, I look into myself for the writing, allowing the sun to sweep through the open space. The deer ranking so high in the constellation of the landscape architecture, that I find myself tongue-in-cheek admiring their carefree stature. Wanting my legs to unfurl, in competition with the deer. The sense of an understated possibility builds up.

Every time I head out into the morning sun, I am searching for a treasure of some sort, great or small, to carry back within. Catching the wave of my breath, slowly lengthening the inhalations and exhalations, feeling renewed. Synchronizing breath with movement, releasing all resistance, I am one with the deer. Moving gracefully through the paths, the bent and broken branches, all of life with ease. Resting on a breath, just a temporary stop, to where I am going... I bask in the flow!

The pulse of my sneakers, feeling just a few more steps removed from the world, I'm left in no doubt that I am a pearl. I immerse myself in the morning air, as the poetic blank slate of the open blue sky seduces my breath. The wind embraces me, orbiting me in flight to foreign places. Two birds take seating near by, taking advantage of the view. Profusion of purple tulips bending ragged in the wind, speak to me of their enduring. Their placid presence beckons me onward.

A trio of squirrels now position along a bend in my path exuding a playful spirit. Placement is key, as my feet infuse with a timeless elegance. My breath embellished by poetic inscriptions, encouraging me to linger on my sweat.

Rustic and refined, thoughts scatter. Nature furthering my sense of anticipation and mystery by revealing only a glimpse of what lies beyond, as I design my own life haven. My mantra offering calm in the center of my composition, executed in brushstrokes of color. For all its solicitude, I find water one of the most enchanting places on earth to linger, as I run towards the river. It is what reflects off the water that sets my journey apart, retracing steps of a passage in my reflection. Looking beyond the reflection, to my more palatable gloss, an inevitable collection of sweat, now a torrid river down my legs. Total immersion in the view of the river, a moody shade of slate and olive, its a long way from the trials and tribulations of life that I come for. Pushing the wind, letting the river flow, as beads of sweat fall deep into its abyss, I watch the river flush away my toxins.

Backwards extension, opening my breath with a deep sun salutation, I expand my arms, and take in breath. Releasing the heaviness I carry on my shoulders, and the prick of the thorn from within. Following in the trust of being re-made, as my run today is exalting. Another day, another step in the journey, my sneakers have not let me down... as the glass of my sweat for today, is left behind at the river's bank.

Today a hush envelops the entire world. Rising early, a few architectural jewels of the landscape rise with me, encased in drips of morning dew. Everybody wanting to go to heaven, as I head out the door, putting two feet on the ground, I am already there. The air is comfortably warm on my flesh. A small flock of birds fly over my head, revealing pale undersides as they turn in unison, flashing against the darkened sky like an animated constellation. They land further down on the field, retreating as they probe the ground. Tiny flecks of morning mist wash down, tracing patterns on my face. My limbs are loose, and skin now salty. The birds now diving for worm delights. My mind rises and dives with the birds. In this elemental place I become less encumbered. I shed something of myself against the living world and rest my eyes on a horizon unmarred by human will. I begin to remember who I really am, as I revel at the thought of the sun, the tug and sway of the sea, the cooling breeze on a summer's night.

Something shifts. I feel strangely buoyant, as a tide rushes in, never revealing more than I want to show. Weathered shutters serve as a colorful accent to the window of my life. Lace curtains now blowing in the breeze allowing fragments of light in. My sneakers have their own personality, bold, independent, thorny and demure, delicate and serene, clustering colorfully as they hold my thoughts.

The restorative presence of water in the air, hastens my relaxation in tempo and breath. The timeless enchantment of the deer captivates my eye, creating a focal point, enveloping them in a skirting of greenery of the grass. A refreshing cocktail of beaded sweat trickles down my cheek, as it makes its way to my lips. Being seduced into a worry-free, unreal state for a time, real life roaming, a gesture of pure abandon, without any calculation or fear.

A run is an adventure in another world, for me a paradise. Engaged in a prolonged arduous exertion, under the guidance of my feet. Propelled by some symbiotic force. From ordinary, suddenly I am in open sea, taking flight and achieving distances thought unattainable.

Subscribing to the idea that challenges are opportunities to design life anew, with the stone, brick, and smooth river rock of our choosing. My breath opens up to a colorful palette, as I look at my canvas and begin to paint my life. Each inevitable stumble onto a deserted shore, leaves me breathless and panting.

Rain is pouring down, as I dip my heart into its stream. Effortless drops take hold of my sneakers.

Seasons of life connected by pathways. My sneakers an outlet for my avid focus, not only expands life, but blurrs the lines between nature and existence. Delighting in a multitude of visual and sensory experiences. Captivated by soothing sounds of the waterfall from the sky, leading to a meandering path of seasonal tulips and daffodils. Running the grounds of my color garden, a watering can held above, sprinkling fresh life into me with grace and finery. Color palette softens with the soothing counterpoint of new foliage, a gray green hue of sage. Enlightening the view from within, showcasing an exquisite picture in a cordial glass, exuding elegance in an etched-glass decanter breathing new life into an empty memory with a spray of blissful architecture. Memories, the most utilitarian, are elevated to works of art weathered by the storms. Imagination takes flight.

Memories occupy places in our hearts well out of proportion to their size. Just as you re-cut the stem of a flower so it can soak up water, you replenish a breath to soak up life. Firm petals and buds just opening, suit the character for scale and proportion for memories to be lost in. Creating a harmonious whole with the help of serene shades of green, my sneakers and memories make peace. Continually fascinating and therapeutic, the power of nature evokes a multitude of human emotions. Rain pouring down, washing my eyes to see, a contemplative reflection pool now surrounding my feet. My legs conquering each step, as breath opens up on the taste of rain and fresh morning air. Beating of my heart, now rhythmic to my feet, as nature washes over me. My sneakers, running dialogue with my thoughts, glass bead raindrops, additions to my jar. Kicking off sneakers and melancholy thoughts, I stand here soaked in the rain.

Every run in every season is an adventure. However, spring and summer surrounded by a profusion of sprightly blooms is most perfect for me. My sneakers and I lost in a quiet repose on the hill overlooking the blaze of spring hues, broken only by the tinkling music of dripping dew centered among the blooms.

Soothing green and blue, to exuberant pink and yellow, painting a harmonious living portrait. Like a painter's canvas, coming to life with an inspired imagination, executed with artful brushes of color, my breath awakens me. Tranquility takes flight in a garden of white and green, while saturated pinks and purple tongues set a vibrant stage

I am drawn to. The greatest gift of my run is the restoration of my senses.

Weaving a rich tapestry of texture and thought in the multidimensional composition, my colorful garden of a life. Green is always a soothing constant, unifying surrounding shades within my greater landscape. The peonies and bleeding hearts of spring, their perfume floats and fills the air. My sneakers run through the enchantment. Yellow brightens the landscape, as the early risers, daffodils and crocus lend extension to my space. The symphony of color entraps my vision, the contrast dazzling my eye a calming effect takes over my soul.

The birds take bath in the rippling of a stream, echoing the tranquil nature

of the water within. My sneakers recede
against the living patchwork of color,
with an energy that uplifts me solitude
and sanctuary, my private getaway. The
hectic pace of life now slowed to a
soothing cadence, where tranquility
reigns amid sun-kissed aspirations. The
only sounds that permeate the air are
the sweet serenade of my feathered
friends, the whispering of the trees, and
the trickling tempo of the stream.

My sneakers adjusting to the restful
sights and sounds, inviting moments
of quiet reflection, replenishing my
weary breathe. The outdoor sanctum
has the power to transport me to a
calm oasis. My heartbeat resounds in
the air while I rest amongst the breath
of nature.

A light beginning to my day that
gently tempts my appetite. Parsley,
rosemary, thyme, and mint combine
to flavor the colors of the field

up ahead of me. I linger long, savoring
the first fresh tastes of spring
scents, and sensibility, knowing roses
don't always take care of the mending,
that sometimes, it is in the breath,
a tear left in the rain, or, perhaps,
the hope is in the ending... watching
twinkling stars in the one life that
we are given.

Swallows flying over a sun filled
land, in search of spring and violets.
Diverse plantings along my path gives
opportunity to pause and appreciate
the view. Coordinating colors, as the
moisture from their tongues extends
onto their petals, as my sneakers tip
toe through the tulips. In the shade,
a weeping crocus designed to invoke
serenity. As thoughts unwind, and the
wind prevails, my pace conjoins my
breath. The red robin clinging to my
every word, a burn of fantasy, or chosen
melancholy, left to his wonder. In

fantasy, red robin and I, both take flight. I am ensconced in a dream complete with it's own white picket fence, relaxing on the balcony.

A wall of sun angles down. The world smells of sea salt and endless summer. My priorities align. Drifting into my breath I am absorbed by the lightness of the day. A mortared fieldstone path extends around my perimeter carrying away the sins that once took over me. Besides the scarlet sunset, besides the sea and the rain, besides the wind and the sun, there is much more for me to understand on the cusp of my breath, a crossroads between hope and fear. Surrendering myself to the wind I am a kite in flight.

My colors are that of every rainbow I have ever seen, and every sunset my eyes have taken rest upon. Sun in full bloom, I run mercifully toward home, as the wind presses the sweat close to

my flesh. Sneakers are harnessed in
the dressing of my water vapors. Wind
stained eyes with a permanent tearing,
as my sleeve soaks up the excess. I am
surrounded by cool air as I float out
to the island I anchored just off shore...
my mantra, forgiveness. My eyes open up,
it is I that I saw breathing in the cool
air of an existence, and the peace that
I sought. My sneakers, kicked off at the
door, adding more miles to my journey.

    Mingling easily with the surrounding
pleasing budding of the trees and the
daffodil parade. Clouds in concentric
circles float above me, against the
undressed gray of the skyline. Natures
rushing waterfall soon dominates.
Finding solace overhead, a peaceful private
atmosphere, as my sneakers unleash along
the path. Branches hang casually over my
path, releasing a pungent fragrance as I
pass by. Water courses through a narrow
channel wrapping around the trees. The

balance of warm and cold extends down
my legs, carved from my thoughts and
accessed via my breath as a strong breeze
ensues. An inside, outside connection,
continually brings in the fire of life.

My run becomes an instant piece
of art, giving admiration to my own
stone smooth worn surfaces. Every
step of my journey reveals a new view,
as I wrap around my breath. Tall trees
in a meditation garden, creates coveted
shade. Highlighting favorite memories
while respecting nuances of the faded
ones. My drone of thoughts peacefully
now dissolve in the gentle splashing of
the dropping of the tree buds in the
water, now cascading over rocks. Breathe
softening the strong angles of existence;
I happily take root at the waters edge. A
retaining wall built with multiple tiers,
making room for lost memories to have
a space to come home to. Created mostly
out of reclaimed cast-offs of other
people's memories, not my own.

I close my eyes again behind the
blindfold, and let myself go sensually
to a Caribbean beach, lost, half
naked, pebbles beneath my feet. My

body conforming to the heat and the relaxation as I lie in the sand, on my flesh the border between the water and the air. I can hear the blue-green ocean still washing ashore, a marimba down the beach playing the beat of my heart... my sneakers and I, in seclusion, in another time and place...

Flanking the roadway, tulips now weave through the fence. Tucked into a small plateau on the side of the hill, a petunia garden. Annual and perennial flowers planted in inviting drifts to help secure the hillside. Something in the air attracting a bountiful of small flying insects, as I navigate around the swarms. The insects not a friendly companion for this morning's run, actual intruders. I much prefer the symphony of color and texture of the flowers. Full sun, I mingle freely.

Symmetry reigns. A cast off of

nature's water becomes my meditative reflecting pond. Everything held together in pleasing harmony of color and scents, letting go of the potential feeling of chaos. Diamond patterns on the pond, forming curvaceous silhouettes against the backdrop of the sun. The deer flashing a conspiratorial smile in my direction. Infusion of liquid sunshine sprays down on me, a deluge of sweat transforming my legs to a glistening sheen. Adult – only secrets pour out from within, as I indulge myself in my perfect themed sanctuary.

A mortared-stone foundation, a wraparound fence of secluded retreat, aged and rooted in my sneakers. My breath now softening to a looser unprimed character. Curving garden beds create islands of color in the sea of green grass I now run through. The perfection of life is all in the fantasy, not in the perfection. It is the stones walls, and guarded gates, cracked interiors, and secret corners we share with no one. That is the making of a life. Those that claim perfection are simply hiding the truth. Truth be told, the journey is all the mortar and glue that hold together our accumulated existence of days and moments. It is the parade of endless colors that make for a colorful life. The black and white of safe harbors is not living, it is a fantasy pursued. The sorrows, the pain, the love is the journey of a life!

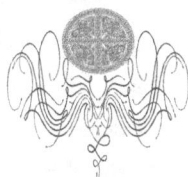

A run into the hills on a cloudless morning, treated to a dazzling mosaic. A bird's eye view of a perfected sun salutation, as the sun appears up over the treetops, the bird's hillside perch, an alluring location. Sun crisp, shedding inhibitions, sneakers imparting a rhythmic instruction, I sidestep an opportunity to run in the mud. As my body heats up, and feet begin to dance in my sneakers.

Sneakers telling a riveting story of an ill-fated passage, their can-do spirit informs my every moment.

Drunk on my breath, sprawled in the warming sun, feet guiding the way, battered but intact, buzzing with energy. This day exudes the ambiance of a summer forthcoming. Watching me through nature's curtain-less window, as I settle into pace, applause explodes from the blue jay. Recognizing me as a solitude seeker, he imparts flight.

Tasting salt, I indulge myself on my sweat. Heat of the sun now cascades across my flesh, as if a whisper is caught in the breeze. Cinnamon, oregano, ginger, red pepper rosemary, thyme, turmeric, all the earth tones of nature surround today.

Sneakers now lead me in the direction of choosing, as I find my mantra in the gurgling of the stream. Water running over rocks in a gully trickling down, as my sweat trickles and mixes in its purity. The feel of the heat, outpouring of sweat, release in my worries onto the pavement. Wide open today, to the warmth that the air is offering. A banquet long overdue, as I lavish in the feast.

Air presses against my chest, fragile, innocent, safety for an instant. Sweetly, I surrender. Wings reaching, glances teaching, judgmental standing in the offerings of the trees, as the air today, is healing. Picking and chooses which ones stay, memories always inside of me, my sneakers have a corner of their own. Letting go of the misery, I have my eye on the enemy in another life tearstains on my eyes, from the places I have wandered to. Divine intoxication, as the red robin zips past my shoulder. Riding past the abyss into which time has fallen into on this day. Bring on the rain, the cleansing of my breath, a little reckless, a little righteous, yet glimpses of archaic wonder all around me. Landing near a puddle, the bird has no fear, no tears, as he drinks from the rain's pleasure. The rain now washes away the sweat, as the sweat infuses with the rain, inspiring peaceful reflection. Cut from pink sandstone are my perfected versions of dreams, an undeniable life – list of thoughts, destinations, places, and people. The pale pink and greens of my thought stands neatly against the slate-gray facade of the morning sky. Flawlessly executed drops of rain rest on my nose. Sneakers, squishy wet, my own case study of comfort.

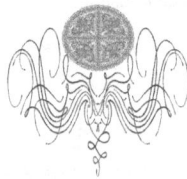

My run intrudes on a blissful procession of budding trees and blooming ever so slowly flowers, drifting on the wings of the birds delighting in the fanfare. The fields as a bed linen layered in wildflowers and crocus. A floral palette of purple, yellow, and deep pink begins at the beginning, a place that consumes all my light. Liquid gold pours down from above, I thrive in a curious space of my own creation, letting the sun's heat absorb me. Deciding to focus on two of my strengths, my capacity for

vision, and philosophical thought, I
float amongst my castle in the air.
In the air allowing the foliage and
flowers that grace the garden beneath it
to enchant with refreshing serenity.
Recognizing graces received and challenges
accepted, of opportunities missed or
seized. Intermittently catching the
glint of sun, the crystals falling upon
me like fractured jewels.

A small mouse scampers past the
wall, as a squirrel encourages the race.
My breath deepens, pores open up, oxygen
flows, ligaments extend and release
with each step of my sneaker, as I
course along. In my castle, Andrea Bo
celli plays, and wine flows in rivers.
Entirely light by candles, the air soon
grows stiffly hot. A candle caresses me.
My run paces with my life, a calculation
of movements, expectations and
assumptions. Revising my perception, for
a few fleeting moments, nothing to hold
onto, thinking about it, breaks it to bits.

Old trees shading brick sidewalks, history revealed in spades. I take off down M street, toward that temple of white. Dimly intending to confront the bone truths of my existence today, through the marriage with my sneakers, my sidekick, my confidante, my partner in excess at times. Pacing past brownstones with big French doors, leading open to gardens of a parade of colors, an almost hand painted fabric pattern. Deciding it must be someone very creative and open minded living there. Cherry Blossom petals scatter the earth's surface. The atmosphere of this place is one of soft enchantment, periodically spiked with elegant drama. Still chilly, the sun has pierced the gray skies, looking decidedly more picturesque than yesterday. My sneakers surrounded in almost every direction by sapphire glinting water and atmospheric architecture. Without a doubt, one of the most therapeutic runs, gazing at the water, all earthly worries a million miles away. It's an instant balm for my soul. Blowing off any of my journey's remaining strains of cobwebs, I am soon happily replete.

Stresses of my journey, immediately eased, by the glittering calm of the river up ahead. Framed by tall silently swaying trees, and renaissance greenery, the journey has the restorative calm I could wish for. Meditate awhile amidst the formal shrubbery and the soft sounds of burbling fountains, worth spending some time here to drink in the magnificent detail upon the collapse of my breath, then head back towards the river.

My entrancement on my breath, a solitude of comforting, as the glass river adjusts it's coloring to the opening skies. An invitation, for me, to adjust my view, balancing the strength of integration in wavelike pulsation of breath, as I travel the passageway of a journey... a bead of sweat escapes to the river, as I watch the glass bead sink, turning to sapphire...

Cherry trees soften the contour. The interim circles are full of floral plantings and marble statues. The striking pink and white buds strike the deep blue sky in contrast. The view imputes my run. The heat on my arms, the sound of the water from the fountain, with reluctance I hedge forward. The flavors and ingredients of this morning dictate a soft, delicate touch. The delicacy mirrored against he facade of the strength of the physical stone monuments off in the distance. Aromatic, the scent lingers at my nose, the cherry blossoms, surely the star of the show, the greenery the supporting cast, not to mask or overshadow.

Drenched in a humid perfusion of self - inflicted wetness, orchestrated by the obligatory breath of the morning humidity, an unforgiving sweat. Every run invites change on the onset of it. Heat fluidly on my back, the river channels down my spine, giving me directions by landmark, as I circumvent through the streets. The moment I first experience the quietude of the gardens, my sneakers beg for more. Postcard-perfect views lends to seclusion in the shade of the monuments. Ambling along, where

interpretive displays depict a history.
The surrounding grounds, a paradise, tidy
rows of flowers, infused with a detail
bursting with color. My legs, open to
nature's suggestion, as to which direction
next. The parks are filled with a studied
variety of trees, all planted centuries
ago. This city is a big book in leather
binding, each page illuminated with a
colorful sketch. The drawings neatly
annotated, more than fulfilling the
visual promise of my trip. A hodgepodge
of current affairs and ancient history,
wealth and poverty, all jumbled as one.
Dozens of elegantly carved statues are
amid public spaces, cracked facades, an
edge, a sense of history. A touch of
collusion riddles between past and
present, as I collide along with the
view. The temple that appears like a
beacon off cobbled street, the white
stone pillars integrated by decades of
alliances and history. Running through
the street, the temple gives me an
immediate visual understanding of what
characterizes it. A perfect conspiracy,
treasured for it's ever changing occupants.
An array of shaded purple sets off my

breath, as the garden of peonies, so simple, almost vogue, pulls my legs in its direction. Home appears like a varied country than the land I am in today.

For this morning, the streets of DC captivate my legs, my breath, my senses, a mantra revealed as I stretch the line of ligaments that run down my calf. For here, nature provides a deeper fuller color of greens, purples, whites, pinks, yellow, and the intrusion is breathtaking. Kicking off my sneakers, maintaining the whiff that lingers at my nose... cherry blossoms, or simply the festival of my own flight.

Perhaps, my own temple of Zeus.

Latching on to synchronicity, the legs begin to flow. Trees whisper in the breeze. It is chaos not pattern which dictates, a turkey fanning out it's array of colors, glass birds atop a tree, statuettes of deer frozen in compromising positions. Nature shuns

the linear and the expected. Onto
the wooded path, the ceiling sparkles
with a myriad of glass beads, as the
dew restfully clings to the treetops.
Nature's illustrations made actual in
the blink of my eye. Each inevitable
stumble with nature leaves me on a
deserted shore. Canvassing the map
ahead, a sinuous ribbon of sky peeks
down over my shadow, as it unfolds
before me. The squirrels scamper back
and forth, resembling nothing less than
an unsupervised kindergarten recess, far
less sensitive to subtlety, than I. A
less marked path, finds a chipmunk
sinking into a deep velvety armchair of
crocus a blissful quiet morning opens
along my path.

Alice in Wonderland whimsy mixes
the flowerbed colors, with the rocks
as earth-toned chairs, as the greenery
of the lawns encroach in abundance
around me. Having the sense of being in
a remarkable moment in time with
stillness and light, my breathe escapes
me, as I labor up the hill of my ascent.
Making changes to my stride, I navigate
through the trees, which quickly form

archways I run through. The unruly foliage sets up like a wall. Order, or the progressive lack of it, is another of nature's directional devices. As my life, appears linear and well trimmed as well, it too, has had a lack of it at times. The arched trees catch the light, drops dramatic shadows over me. My run becomes meandering now, less formal than the challenge of the hill. Almost home, the path widens to accommodate a stone clearing, it's spare but elegant furnishing, an enormously large rock, first glance it becomes the resting spot for my sneakers.

Shaded from the morning sun by a canopy of rain, moisture at my lips, as I drink first and think about later, sweat or rain? Birds gossip on a bench, I lean in as I pass, easily seduced by the notion of their secrets. Lighting a fire, now quickly burning out of control in the abyss of my breath, my legs take off in flight?

Morning dew teardrops sit as capsules on the blades of grass. Broken and unchained, now breaking through, sunshine arriving at last. A wealth of daffodils, now soak in the first morning rays. Leaving everything outside of me, I break off into a run. I immerse myself in poetry, with it, everything is found. When you break it down to every word, every dance, it all resounds back to nature. Life a profound mere mimic of it all. Quietly communing with nature, lost in a silent meditative look at the patterns of the peeping clouds. Immersed in the splendor of the poetry.

Earliest emergence of my legs since late fall, as I am in shorts this morning. My yoga colliding with my running is now visible in my calf with each stride. Bending forward, downward, head to knee, the yoga ever captivating the line of ligaments in my calf. Legs run free of all layering. Sweat absorbed into flesh before it even beads. Legs glisten under the sheen of the wetness. Having allowed for dormancy, the curtailed blood flow and slowed respiration that sustained the crocus over the cold winter, also sustained me. Now, with fleeted passion, I open mouthed, release all my dormancy, and soak up as much air as I can take in.

In a total release of breath, my lungs are restored to the openness of the warmer weather. The trees are rich with chatter and unexpected alliances, amid surprising acts of aggression, as a blackbird lays claim to a branch. The sparrows, regarding with a strange mixture of affection and trepidation, fly off. An element of self-protection, I am sure. Achieving temporary harmony through eternities of time, favoring an undisturbed spot atop the rock. I watch this coexistence of visual strength and physical fragility, existing before me. I am running through the mighty evergreens, which shelter it all.

My path now canopied by trees and lined with roots, with constraint transitions from dark to light, as the sky is unclear as to how to behave. Intuitively nature knows the proper location for each element of its landscape, easily making changes to redirect my sneakers. A renaissance of art and design, gentle paced over the small stones, as even small stones can be obstacles I internalize. The black bird attempting to label me, trying to ignore, hiding my pretend, he only scratches the surface of who I am.

The sparrow, turns around, picks me up on guided wings, bringing me back to my place of grace. The place, along my journey, where my breath is all I hear, my sweat is all I taste, as my legs lift me effortlessly back from the satiric novel, a painful episode. The zen quality of my outdoor run, in this moment in time, has never felt better, as the grace of one sparrow, carries my burdens, my sneakers, and I, now home...

The sun has not yet come up, but my sneakers are calling the austerely landscape transitioning as seamlessly from night to day, as season, to season.

Swinging elegantly on my shoulders, a bead of early sweat. A combination of Zen and pure poetry, called "Zoetry." Morning, my favorite time, air is crisp and cool, and the lawn is dressed with clouds today, bathing it with a frequent rain. Keeping it perpetually painterly green, seemingly to blend organically with natural beauty. My path begins beneath the rustling canopy of tall trees, and the sounds of birds, whispering secrets, as I pass. While reflecting on the scale of the undertaking, a long uphill climb ends at the windswept crest, with a sweeping view of the riverfront. My legs mimic the tree, the flower, the wind. Thinking of nature as a sort of divine intervention. Always serving up life on a silver plate, always leaving me, inspired. I am given a whole new infusion of energy, delighted to eavesdrop on the bird's conversation. I am focused on my mission, serenity now. I concentrate on the surrounding sounds: the trickle of the rain, the rhythmic whisper of the birds, the strains of sweat carried on my breeze. The essential elements of my run are all in place. I brace myself for the interruption, as the deer dart by, at one point I think I hear them giggle at me.

I am impervious to embarrassment, as the world becomes my catwalk, tying up my shirt, so skin is exposed to air. My body, once again, entangled with my breath. The quenching of my navel, as it becomes the cup for the river of my sweat. Stepping from path to pavement, I loose all of my magical powers, like Superman, returning from Krypton. My fantasy landscape takes rest for another day. My sneakers, wet with aroma of the salt of my wounds, as the cup overflows from my navel...

More open to being influenced by nature. My legs are the trunks, from which my branches truly grow. You can make it through anything, if you know it is temporary, becomes my mantra, as I push up the steep incline. My sweat sprinkles what is the equivalent of fairy dust on me, as I pace myself feverishly. The Red Robin leaves his perch in the tree, flies by me side, grabbing hold of my sneaker, unfurling my laces, as he picks me up in flight. A beautiful display, as we fly across the sea, breath falls to the earth like a crashing wave. All of passion, all of sin, taken by the wind, rides a breeze in fulfillment. As the robin opens his wings, and carries me up, he drinks from my sweat, an ever-ending cup. Existing in my own time zone, yet not quite alone, layers of intrigue, as the robin waves me on. Nature answers my request, a release of toxins, and medicinal property of my run.

Sweat begins to flood from my every pore. The first morning taste of diluted sweat, not yet absorbed by the sun. Sharp, salty, refreshing even, leaving a sensation on my tongue. For now, I pause, and let the sweat clear my mind and quench my palate. As my sweat drips down upon a crocus, on the edge of the field, the Robin seemingly to say to me, "If you do not nurture it, do not expect it to live." The crocus is in a permanent state of relaxed napping. The smell hits me, the whiff of pine chips surrounding wind bent trees. The romance still lingers between the Robin and I, hoping the euphoria lasts the rest of the day. It is human nature, isn't it? Needing to belong to something greater than myself, I have the vague but comforting conviction that I am a pearl on that iconic beach, amongst the sea glass, shells, and salty fresh air. The red robin taking rest on a straggling bush, clinging to it's few wiry branches. My rather transparent inclination is to stop and watch, and rest beside him. Pausing...

Recognizing the past, like the present, is shaped by flawless flesh and blood circumstances, sometimes, beyond our control. The climax of that final winded breath, the final puzzle piece. Spring has at last, been delivered by nature. In the envelope opening of the sun on my face, slight wind from east to west, or is it west to east, swirling around me, wilting away the perspiration on my flesh. Warm and radiant, tree buds nourished by the snow showers of yesterday, fueled now by an emerald green lawn. Sights and sounds, encompass my spirit, the essence of a spring, firm in it's standing. I soak up its endurance into my legs, firmly grounded in my own standing. A restless bravado encourages my legs up the hill.

The deer have a predilection for me now. Nothing of note seems to escape them, surely, not I, this morning. The sun imbues me with a quiet suffuse warmth. Working as a form of energy conservation for my body. The itinerary offered up to me today, a view along the river, charming and restlessly entrancing from the edge. My reflective sense is in the water, providing the most physical and umbilical bond with nature. My personal interest in bodies of water began long ago, living along the coastline. The spectacle of different hues of Caribbean greens to inky blues, a near pristine natural environment.

Stretching out through my legs, I feel the suppleness down my spine. Warrior pose perfected, as the river is my mirror for alignment. The fluidity I take from the water. The illusion I can float above it, or dig down deeper into its depths.

Finding the river, and my run today, seductively placid. The endless monologue between myself, and my sneakers, ushers me home. Up once, from where I came, looking back at the river, I straddle the crest of the hilltop. The chance acquaintance of the bluebird, eloquently accompanying me home.

Winters weight, once breaking the limbs of the tree, today, now only a fading memory on my sneakers. The tree once snapped under winter's weight, the silence of the words, broken, no one heard. I hurdle over the twigs and branches, now outstretched on the ground, beneath my feet. The floating cascade of white cotton balls from above, no longer holds reveal, as they dissipate on the ground. The final release, winter trying to contain her, not break her, providing forbearance, as spring slips through. For me, as well, the forbearance, as I slip through. From the depth of frost to the first awakening of spring. Each run produces a beautiful idea colorful and metaphoric, ever establishing me the writer, with my sneakers, in the firmament of the morning. I am drenched in sweat, on the drunkenness of my own breath. I am envisioning a barrier reef, jutting out of the ocean, as far as my eyes will lend me. Barefoot, the coolness of the sand now filters through my toes. The sand, allowing me to retrace the footprints of my run, as it holds the pattern of each step. Making a mental note, to add this place to my bucket list, ever growing. I return to the disintegrated relationship between winter and spring.

The deer today, assumes the role of caretaker of the woods. The molting of his coat is his unearthing into spring. He stands before me, in all his bareness, his lack of movement, waiting for my reaction. Not that I will ever tire of the sight of him, I run on. The road up ahead leads me home.

Kicking off my sneakers at the door, my hand dislodging a gritty piece, silver and glimmering from between my toes, the glass sparkles drop to the floor. Giving largely to the suggestion, perhaps, of the sand from the barrier reef.

The morning is bathtub warm, wind is slack, giving my flesh an almost instantaneous glossy appeal. As I reach out to touch my hand to a crest of air, I feel my fingers slip along my invisible wall of breath. Birds gather to watch me ride the waves of heat, as my arms suspend themselves in drifts. Morning's waters strip through my flesh, creating small ribbons of cliffs inching down my shoulders to my navel. Summers heat shifting my landscape yet again.

My architecture in constant renewal of itself, imagination collides with idyllic thought, wanting to be covered in a fanning of palm trees. The short-lived blooming of spring flowers representative of my common belief in the transience of all things, as the flowers drag their tongues collapsing under the heat. In a fumbling flurry I de-clothe, stuff my textiles into my waistband, considering full nudity as an option as flesh melts upon the black pavement.

My hands hold my spirits, as my eyes hold my secrets, a thirst for meaning and purpose, as always, to life's unfolding. Listening to the sounds of silence and discerning the rhythm that has become my dance. Breath and mind open up with an erotic tendency, further dancing into a seduced state of mind.

The birds, the trees, everything seems to resonate my energy. Silence becomes my harmonious state of mind and sated pleasure.

Water runs through the hose of my pores, as my eyes fix on the chest of stolen gold skyward.

Meditating through my sculpture garden, bearing homage to the goddess of moonlight for the breaking of a new day. Ushering myself into the hushed interior of nature, I feel as though I should whisper. This morning my floor-to-ceiling mirror of existence, the air so hot I soon can't feel my lips, as salt courses through my veins. Humidity, as a peppery red spice hangs from the trees. Concentrating on surroundings sounds, heat releasing a lot of emotions. Temperature keeps rising, in a sauna, in this gilded moment in time, my overheated, dehydrated body conforms to the beating of my heart, then finally relaxes. My hydrotherapy now making me putty in the hands of my inner thoughts. What I have learned in my life, is bittersweet, mercilessly all things come to pass. Expectations and assumptions, most of us aspire to such unbridled joy, a washed in flower petals, channeling my inner artist, as I construe poetic verse of breath across the sinuous blue velvet ribbon of sky. Nature providing the fabric for the tapestry I weave, as my feet crisscross through the wooded path, foliage draping me into seclusion.

Just whom I thought I was, and who I thought I had to be, fills in the gaps belonging to my transition. My tongue now searching for water in the mirage of heat, as eyelashes veil my eyes from the sting of the salt. Self derived borders of personally constructed suffering, as I close my eyes to better see, that wherever I go, there I am. Solitude, my morning companion, profoundly empowering manifestations of human heart, suggesting I do not always have all the answers.

I breath in the heat of the day

leading further ponder for tomorrow, as the silence of my words and the taste of peppery sweat saturate my lips.

I will swathe myself in shades of pastels, as the brilliance of the sun streams through my bedroom window. Easily seduced by the sun and the unpretentious intrigue of it's heat on my flesh, I strip from covers and enter my "place of peace."

Life is about moments, as much as the accumulation of those moments, as they form us all as individuals. Becoming a compiled substance through many trials and tribulations, and maintaining the harmony- within. Life for myself holds a treasure trove of unique and distinctive offerings. Learning and accepting, how to properly divide and separate, gently thrusting all the experiences apart, has become a very long and mindful accolade of who I am. Tickling air, with its long handle and extending fingers, against my face each morning, becomes my own sense of religion. My method of meditation allows uneasy thoughts to run free, wherever my breath takes them. My methodology of prodigious memory contending with my thin slices of fragmented lost memory becomes heavy clay I sculpt poetry from. No question, there is a constant stream of thought each day, catching me, at times, off guard. Memories spent as some lie dormant, others, self-sewers where ever their seeds have drifted; encouraging them to clamber through my shadows, transposing them into black and white photography, studded with tiny stones, that serve to radiate heat and reflect the sun into my vines. Mesmerized by slices of personal history, all of which are inexorably intertwined, as their colors are not yet set apart. Looming against a sky of provincial blue, words of earlier echo in my brain.

Understanding what it means to loose successive years of life, not being able to retrieve the memories. Tasting the idea of letting go, in every sip, the gathering of wisdom in every glass of morning dew.

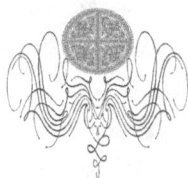

Epiphanies come un-jarred as I troll through memories. Snapping a series of life photographs as my low tide has passed, and the sand has become softer. Sand- clouds sit.

Now captured, positive vibrations, as hardships are worn as a badge of honor. Underwater, a hermit crab trundles along the bottom in its periwinkle shell, crossing a backdrop of rocks splotched with pink, green, and orange algae. I, in my colorful breath, pick up the colors. Common seagulls cry overhead. I stop to watch them hover over the water. White and black caps and brilliant orange beaks, they fold their bodies into arrows of hunger and plunge into the waters. Every so often, one rises into the air with a small, silver fish. My breath rises and dives with the birds. Giggling at my feet as they splash among the waves. In

this elemental place of water and sand,
perhaps I become less encumbered. I
shed something as I brush up against the
tide, resting my eyes on a horizon unmarred
by human spirit and will. I begin to
remember who I really am: a writer who
revels on her back in the sun, the tug
and sway of the sea, the cooling breezes.

The beach is a place of paradox, it
smacks of eternity, yet the landscape is
always in flux with the tides. My feet in
wet sand are now reflecting towering
shadows, as though I am walking on the
sky. Running along the tide's advance and
retreat, as my toes probe the wet sand
for small treasures of sorts. Planting
my eyes like a set of binoculars in the
washed-up seaweed, a horseshoe crab
blending into the surroundings, even on
my bright exposed beach. Sand fleas ping
around my ankles as I search the tangle
of seaweed and sea grass, for the sea
glass I am so longing for. Nowhere does
time feel shorter and more precious
than on my beach on a clear spring
morning. The sun is audacious, as the sea
holds the winter chill, a reminder of
what is past. The long curve of beach

beckons me into its distance, as waves crash on shore, tossing back a salty mist. Wanting to crawl into a conch shell and allow breath to harmonize with the sound of the waves. I hold the tiniest piece of pale thyme sea glass on the sliver of my finger, careful to control it's fragility, as tide rushes in, washing my sneakers out to sea, barefoot, leaving imprints in the sand. I find my way, to where once I began with honey-amber sin kissed skin and salted breath, closing my eyes to see...

Holding round table discussions with birds over fruity sunset colored rum mornings. Sun kissed flesh now shedding inhibitions as I weave through a path, imparting rhythmic breath upon instruction. After a harrowing maiden voyage I have been transposed to this time and place. Sprawling in the warming sun, catching a breeze, gliding east. My pace picks up, as my sails unfurl, as

breath flashes silver in the air once
more. The quiet charm of the secret
retreat of rising early beguiles me, as
much as my bird friends alike. The humid
air and silent surroundings suggest of
the most minimal clothing adorning
the body. As I soak in the salt, a hawk
interrupts the reverie. Whispering in
the breeze, my breath becomes a stately
entryway for crystal clear waters to
lap my shores. Picture perfect beginning
a scarlet bird eyeing my view. Stray
chipmunks scurry across my path. Deer,
in disbelief, as if I were adorned in pink
and purple polka dots and knee high
socks. Running thoughts beyond the
cradle of the sun, my personal safari
into lavish isolation, stumbling onto
distant deserted shores. Virgin territory
I call my own. Then I keep running, and
when I arrive, I see it, wild and
beautiful, my future as a sand angel
lying on a beach of pearl, angling out my
arms as gilded wings, without another
human soul in view. Enjoying a perfect
run on my ultimate beach.

Holding the illusion of sand between
my toes, and the mirage of sea salt

quenching my flesh, as the blue-green ocean washes over my naked body, nestling around each pearl droplet of sweat, as my only loin cloth washes out to sea. The starfish are now twinkling at me in unbridled confidence, burying troubles in the sand. Kicking off sneakers, in the calm beating of my heart and the sweet indulgence of yet, another day, melding seamlessly with the low-key intimacy of the boutique sun, sipping sweat on morning infused cocktails, stripping down, focused on this morning's mission, eyes closed... the rhythmic whisper of serenity... as I soak in the bliss, taking rest from the journey...

Smiling, like god is pulling at the corners of my mouth, lecturing myself, stepping out of comfort zones. Granite structures jut from the ground like a majestic bony hand reaching skyward pulling down beams of sunlight. Beams steaming downward as I lavish in content. Making a profound discovery about myself, that the sun really does make a difference in thought patterns. The rain, is a point of contention for me. Life lessons I struggle to hold onto, as they flit away, and dodge around one dark corridor or another. Maybe they are so hard to hold onto because their lessons are so simple... Each moment contains the world.

I wake up early, edit mental images well into the night, as I melt away from the dehydration of this morning's run. My breath serves as a scaffold for flowering vines, suspended in the air amongst the trees, draped in their branches, flaunting exceptionally fragrant and long lasting commentary. Beads of sweat become more adorned jewelry, achieving a temporary harmony. Being here, experiencing time as an infinite present. I stand in my living shrine, breathing in the mystery. One of the reasons I run is to revel in thought. My runs join the disparate pieces, pulling individual thoughts into unified compositions. Seduced by nature's color saturated sumptuousness, my sneakers,

circumnavigating the strolling path,
hurdling over a dry cascade of rocks.

Exactly what defines life? Is it
my abundant imagination that persists
and creates, despite the inevitability
of life's constant change?

For the moment primed by my morning
ritual awakening, ready to receive a softer
unfolding world, I allow myself to
drift into contemplation, as a route
to further evolve. Further finding a place
to call my own, as my pores become the
vessel for my salt drippings.

Acceptance

Sweet indulgence as I allow myself to drift off into the blanket of fog, as I can't see, but only hear. The air defies easy categorization this morning, as it lays heavy on my shoulders and breath, as I expertly attempt to slice through. Playing hide and seek, illusions begin to stray, as a veil of mystery suspends around me, a charcoal gray. Ensconced in the fog my eyesight ends, as I root in darkness, artifacts of places and people fill the corners of my mind.

Feeling the shifting play of humidity dancing on my flesh, as salt beads cling in suspended motion. The overheated crashing symphony runs a river along my body, as fog still shrouds the air. Deer, amused at my entrapment in the fog, stand motionless, eyes fixated on my query as to what to do ? Seeing the barest rose now beginning to bud, the contradiction between beauty and the prick of the thorn, as I wonder if we don't all bleed sometimes from other people's wounds. Harboring the infliction, as if it were our own.

The morning's air recedes to a type of quiet, as waterfalls spill over me. Fragmented out to sea, on a wave of breath, red robin perched on a limb sings me lullabies ensuing my breath. My flesh is water – retaining succulent, igniting colors, pink and orange splashes of heat radiate off of me.

Having an eye for the unique, as well as a facility with color and texture, my thoughts become opulent brocaded weaves. My life is not beige it is a tapestry of color, as each day I add to the mural on my interior wall. Coral encrusted undersea canyons accessible only in my dream music weaves through the air in shades of blue and amber.

Blocks of salt coat my flesh, as dried chilies and incense is my premixed potion. Licking the salt I am intrigued. Apple-green French silk meadows adorn perfectly intact beneath a shroud of untamed foliage, giving me permission to be singular, as I wrap my circles of color around me. I see the grace of the human form shadowed, as the physical falls away, and new breath now breathes through me.

Drops of rain on my shoulders die on the pavement. My broken pieces I plant like seeds, wisdom now so far away from childhood.

Rain and wind pit me in a wild place on the edge of darkness. As night fades and sun hollows over the horizon, it's time to dispel the darkness with morning's light. Restrained, creeping up

on me, rolling out around me beneath a
huge sky, vapors of first morning breath.
Languishing on the ferment of thoughts,
wishing away the decay. Natural textures
working with my neutral colors creating
calm, my breath clean and sleek,
shoulders drop as I relax.

Fully embracing natural surroundings,
a bird's song repeats in the background.
Deer having a moment are silhouette
in a spellbinding view, standing at
happily drunken angles on a bed of
meadow. Air tastes bitingly fresh, as
I envision sea salt spray on my flesh,
harboring portraits of waves tingling
at my toes. Draining breath on an
amber colored sunrise, vanilla flavored
clouds float my memory de-kinking
and unwinding. Creating a meditative
nook of thought, soothing repetition of
my steps. In depth conversation with
the birds, gentle detoxification.

Breathing slowly, imagining I am
floating on an unsinkable raft in the
middle of a warm blue ocean, looking up
at a clear blue sky, as sea air bathes my
skin and breath. Saturated with poetic
rushes...

My run becomes my "naked in public."
My mind said not to, but I slowly
disembark, finding myself in uncharted
waters. At first, I began at least wrapped
in a sarong, until I realized I had to be
nude. Yes, nude. No shyness, mandatory
nakedness. Compelling example of
humanness and all that it would bring.
As I stand comfortably naked in front
of hundreds of flesh clothed humans, I
have to admit, the sun, clouds, air on
my skin, all of my skin, feels amazing.

As I lie in warm sand and dribble
out the wording, naked and raw for
all the world to see. Secrets escape
impinging on my layers, a shedding of
my skin, naked beauty the liberation of
my weaknesses. A smooth round perfect
pearl released from the oyster, as the
purity of the thought captures my
breath. Naked with just my personal
string of pearls en-cloaking me, as the
simple element of the pearl becomes
the elegance to my flesh.

Every pearl, a stone encountered,
a hurdle in my path now overcome.
Expanded lungs with each breathe, as I
stand in the naked still air of existence.
Time to stand and stare, air is clear,
clean and lilac scented, creamy yellow
shafts of sunlight spear down through
the cloud wisps in a pale blue sky.

Skinny-dipping into thoughts,
plummeting down into dark turquoise
water. The breeze that blows in coats
my lips in salt. The churning and crash of
my breath sends birds wheeling skyward.
Finding a secluded beach upon which my
pearls and I submerge into the water,
flesh bared to the soul, as the heaviness
of life is shred with my clothes...

Trying to gain footing against my salt
spray of breath, as it serpents into the
air. The morning is mundane, yet magical.
Antique stone blocks forming a wall
beyond the sky, as my sea glass and
driftwood anchor me. Collecting and

arranging thought with reckless abandon, arranging whatever thoughts collide my way, my real journey never in new landscapes, but in having new eyes. A sense of layering from my canopy down to my under plantings, filling in my understory, enjoying the dabbled shade. Fringing the air, drops of my breath take flight. Overrun by floral, as my prettiest ingredient to life in this morning's absence of honey glazed light.

My glass pavilion serenely reflecting colors of the forgotten rainbow, which now holds me. With so many glass walls, I am inside outside all in the same breath. Evolving over time, layer by layer, into a truthful representation.

Speaking of where I have been, and that which has cultivated my journey, always resilient. Approachable to the constantly changing colors of the open sky, an inherent patina of bluestone against charcoal serenity unfolds before me. As I run toward the framed picturesque curve of the river, I am a living breathable art form, glazed over in subdued tones. Conviction, poise, as the dance in my feet embodies such things.

I am running along sea cliffs on a hot summer's day. Sunshine, soft sand, and translucent waters surround me. Already immersed in my morning run, skin radiating heat from last night. I plunge into the sea, in full view of nothing but sky, birds, and sun. The mapping of cold pure sea over me, water runs cool over my eyelids, and winds its way around my body and breath in ribbons of cold current.

Spontaneous naked immersion reacts as a siren like sea of fantasy. The best runs are never planned; they just happen, one moment I am running and the next stripped to the winds, running toward the water, exultingly bear. Standing naked, blow- drying in the breeze. Full moon, early morning, rain, dusk, all collide into one view. Heavy rain opening possibilities, raining so hard that the downpour acts as my cloak.

The inconvenience of rain, being soaked through, disappears when it is just me, naked, and breathing. The feel of the water, fish like sense of gliding, child-like vividness and intensity, purity and playfulness to dancing in the rain. Every rain becomes a little more free and liberating. The pure self conscious poetry preserved, no time for change, water drops evaporating on my flesh against the salt of sweat.

I am a work in progress, air blessedly cool on my breath, pairs of birds escorting me, like a Disney Animation. Meandering slowly back in thought, still pacing to the sound of the waves, and the pattering of rain, the rain, a little escape from everything, as it washes away in streams on the pavement washing away the mud, exposing the heart. The rhythm of movement gives cohesion and clarity to my thoughts. I am myself, alone in the beat and the pulsating of my heart as I breathe.

Feeding my soul, and embracing what I love, indulging in passions, painted bookshelves line my walls, with thoughts spilling from stacks on the floors and tables. Rich paint color, looking up, waiting for the Caribbean sky to open up, and dreams once past to breath and come true. Removing vines from my exterior, trimming my trees, breathing new life into my interior. Peering at each morning from a different angle, as nature offers me options. Going back to roots, uncovering old and worn surfaces, allowing honey infused light to bounce off ocean waves.

Breathe, my livable elegance. The height of my stained glass windows, like a conservatory, I am anchored in the view. Emulating an alluring haven, a reflective romance, and thoughtful repurposing. As an old mirror adding faded presence to life, a reflective crystal chandelier, blends air into a soft golden wheat wall of color. My breath enhanced, the sea flat, ideal conditions for viewing what lies in wait ahead for me.

Soft coral grows from my scalp, sea sponges sprout from my ears. Today, vision transforming a typical run into an unexpected pleasure in the rain, as

my feet plunge into an arena of puddles,
equal part illusion, as it is forgotten
thought.

I elegantly dance in the rain, as fairy
dust cascades from the heavens onto the
pulse of my beating heart, a full morning
of moisture gathering on the trees.
Nurturing and growing my own creative
story, accepting the rain, no longer
feverishly bailing out the river with a
teacup... I am unchained to just be...

Soft color, and relaxed tranquility,
from the outside I am as picturesque
as a storybook, my curved roof line and
diamond - paned windows, enveloped by
a sea of calm. Smoldering coal against
the silk walls of sky, as silk white
gowns of clouds drape down to reach

my breath, as I am excavating into the ground. My corridors and wings allowing thoughts to dispense from place to place. Having a transporting quality, my deliberately chipped walls where imperfection is slightly off, blending seamlessly with my antique. I am imbued with mystery, looking out from my balcony of opera in the mezzanine overlooking my life, a cocoon like separation, a portal to somewhere else, my peaceful sanctuary.

Pale gray walls against scarlet breath, a slightly chilly character to the morning, as droplets cascade. Hanging in suspense as chandeliers in the trees, each bead sitting on a throne of air, indulgent in the stillness each represents. Red robin collides with the vapors of scarlet breath, forming a crimson gold portrait against the charcoal landscape. Legs glistening as my body's dew sits on my flesh, sprinkling salt onto the pavement.

Charcoal portrait shaded and subdued,
as flowers still sleep in last night's
dreams, tongues silent not reaching.
   Sneakers leaving imprints on the
path, as a rain drenches with a soaking,
beautifully encased in crystal drops, my
mosaic surface shimmers under nature's
washing... as I open the door and leave
the veil of rain, there I see the rainbow
so contently hollowed within, as I
breath in... the colors deepen.

   Soaring serenity returns to life
shuttered spirits, revealing the tragedies
that haunt, and the grace found later in
life to accept and express extraordinary
sorrow and loss, pain and healing, self-
evolving. Elegant renderings of travels, a
watercolor and casein image of the sea
and harbor float above me, forming an
exhibit powerful in content and emotion.
As the tide recedes, water's transparency
mesmerizes the transforming of my
thoughts. In the distance silhouetted

against the sky of sea, green and white poetry. The gestures validate the intense preparation of each production, as seagulls take stage holding a mirror up to nature. Flowing into one another, maintaining perfect symmetry and breath infused views, taking elements from nature and bringing the "outside" in. Finding a meaningful patina, admitting that sometimes the decay, has added to my character.

The sky's background, a gloomy shade of gray, resounds of constraints. As creative intuition envelopes me in a mindful scene of sea and beach, loosing the sullenness of the day into a personal watercolor of change. Feet are drenched in the washing, as mud pillars on my ankles, sweat cascading down on me.

Flowers hold out their teacups to accept their fill, as chamomile interprets the taste of the air, as droplets spill in indulgence from the teakettle above. My body is a river, as waves of rain crash onto my shores, adding heaviness to my breath. Self absorbing the rain to cool my flesh,

I pound through the puddles... splashes
of rainbows lean out ahead of me, as
I lean into the colors of stained glass,
the reflection turns a beautiful purple,
as reflection of self becomes one with
the mirage... I breath in, breath out...

Wanting to find a beach gently lapped
by water so clear you cannot tell where
dry sand stops and water begins, the
crystalline waters shimmering in the
twinkle of my eye. Seaweed sprouting
out of places you'd expect to see hair,
as vines entangle my body. Just beneath
the surface, my breath barely speaking.
Shafts of light pierce the gloom of the
sky, where rock and flesh do not block
them, a leap of faith into the heart of
smoldering darkness.

A sense of mystery, as day unfolds,
thoughts today, a sacred place. Sneakers
showered with sweat, thoughts erode by
millenniums of tiny drops of salt laden
effort, in unrecognizable textures and

patterns, as they drench my feet. Shifting air currents revealing the curve of my cheek, as the feather leaf of a nearby tree wipes away sweat encapsulated on my left shoulder, backing out of the trees, turning to the horizon, a technicolor mirage, I lose myself in the moment.

Framed in ornate columns, I am both king and fool, making sense from the bird's expansive gestures, embodiment of philosophy, I'm casting seeds into the wind, as one or two take root in my breath... some prayers finding answers, some prayers never knowing, holding on and letting go...

Delicate gauze hangs down from the sky, clearing mental cobwebs, feeling my heart rate now rise on oxygen infused breath. Leaning into the change, reminiscing on what is being left behind. To be fully alive is to repeatedly be changing, as air shifts on my lace woven skin. Slipping into the skin of the flower, experiencing it's frustrations, as if they were my own. Petals die on the ground, a needed automatic release, for the newest to survive. Change in the shifting...

Heeding the bird's calling, paying attention to the silent places between his words. Show stopping clusters of white flowers are shedding skin, moving forward. As the breeze picks up, petals detach, one by one, transforming crumbled breath to aromatic perfume, smell lingering on my senses. All the thoughts collide that live inside of me, in balletic poised ribbon along the sky. Reaching up, I pull them down, as my legs become extensions of another time and place.

Tears once spilled across a nighttime sky, as the moon has faded to another day of purest serenity. Muted hues, brick walls and a hint of gray skyline, I'm floating, my feet dangling in the calm cool water of breath and air, a massive mural in progress as my paintbrush wrestles with the complexities of human emotion, as simple words set to simple melodies begin to paint. I

gently tread on the painted pathway... as
salt laden droplets imprint each step...

At the interface of runner and
wanderer, my painted silk walls, inside
a brick facade, enter my wounds, along
with a profusion of English roses.
Tide of reality recedes easily enough,
clustering diamonds into a patterned
ornamental rug, twined in life, leaving
imprints on whatever I touch, small
drizzles of color surround me, my
picture frame. Squeezing out the
darkness, I find meaning in odd peculiar
places.

An insistent self proclaimed need
to walk through the mine field,
preserving the fragility of fragmented
glass, carefully filling a jar, piecing
together threads, reshaping a shard
vision. Clearing out life, keeping only
what enhances me, as dusting off wings
makes it easier to fly. Lesson I keep
learning, over and over, this too shall

pass, and when it does, intrusive moments of self – discovery arise.

A squirrel claiming territory from the chipmunk, as chipmunk joyfully aims in pursuit of finer furnishings. Spilling breath into air, the vapor silhouette freezes in time. Profusion of sweat, as a tulip reaches hand up to save me from the drown, quenching it's petals on my water beads. Unable to retrieve completely, my past memory, a key component of that which we are, perhaps, it is the not remembering that makes the essence for a neater life.

Carried by the mystical blue of the sky, powder puffs float above me, sun at my back, as legs unfurl closer to the river, shadow eclipses to reflection, as breath is caught up in the embrace. A near full sun salutation, as I settle into the view, closing my eyes to see, a near complete portrait of me. As sweat drips into the river, and nature and I, for a brief moment, are one.

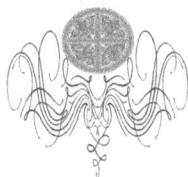

The preservation of the sudden naked instant of contact between night and day arrives, as sun hesitantly rises. A green oasis crisscrosses a footpath, finding refuge to lay aside the chaos of the world. Crimson flower clusters, my breath's focal point. Peaceful, forever calm, and energized. A garden leads entry into a serene, orderly and visually coherent world. A steep winding meadow lined road leads to the sexy shifting of the trees, as they fan their flesh with their foliage, discreet and demure.

Witnessing the rhythm of passing years as plants and flowers come in and out of bloom and leaf, as seasonal displays rotate around my existence. The landscape, my shadow, stealing color from the field, etching out stone after stone of the journey. The curtain now draws on the theater of last night's dreams, as daydreams form my daylight canopy.

Piled in smoldering profusion, flaunting their lurid contents, tulips bask in the sun. Listening to birds, licking off dewdrops, suckling, I begin to grow.

Breath fully inhaled, and folded in my wings. The day clear as fire, the birds sing frail as glass, as deer wait in the grass. A moment or two when self disappears under a cloudless sky. In a moment of clarity I realize fear would eat me up, if I let it, and I could not let it set in. Fear takes us to panic, not power. No longer playing within the boundaries, letting self reside within, curious paradox of accepting myself as I am, and then, change as I will.

Mornings air calm, heartbeat thundering on the lightest breath. Salty sweat covering me in a canopy, favoring a language of spiritual and metaphysical uplift, energy only my sneakers understand. If my run seems like a fantasy, it is because inspiration comes from exactly that: a life dream. Life that is off center, off kilter, implores me to use my imagination. Raspberry, pink, and hues of green shimmer under the sun's light, as

stained glass windows I look through.
Simplicity of nature and the simple
embankment of no clear storyline to the
day, I let my feet paint the poetry...
leading down my passage to another day.

In the background, visible through
my glass walls, life dives and preens.
Seasons change. Inviting lingering
conversation with the birds, enveloping
each of my five senses, providing me
melody on demand, as a glass misting
fountain releases a gentle fragrance
to keep the flowers happily quenched.
Ladybugs flit here and there.
Sitting snug, enclosed by my glass
walls, clearly in my own element,
sinking my roots into a setting where
they are exposed eloquently, personally,
and permanently. Personal portrait
hanging framed by a water view. Burst of
azaleas in first bloom, throwing a few
patches on some life wounds, seducing
myself into an engaging storyline. Life at

times is satirically repetitive. A palette of paint chips, photocopying memories, cutting them out, layered into a life of varied combination. The grace of my human form reflected against the pavement, shadows of a painful gray area, no way not to think about it. Existence marinates, painted in the gray blue of the skyline, patterned fabrics shimmer in the sun. A bird under a tree, sits contemplating the river.

My breath slowly adjusts. I start to feel the spices, blocks of salt encrust my flesh as intense as dried chilies, incense permeates the air, meditative potions. Accustomed to the soaking in my sneakers, as the deluge runs down my legs, as a glistening string of beads substantiates around each ankle. Salt in overload this morning, as breath controls thought. Substantial in appearance but quiet in effect, deer forge for breakfast out on their balcony, unearthing an array of delights.

Tulips in a soldier's stance are fearless in juxtapositions of time and place, as are memories of old and new. Pressed against my glass wall, sweat

frames a personal portrait, as I become
drunk on the intoxication. Convinced
I have just entered a new dimension,
sipping wine on the French Riviera, the
music sultry and serene, taking breath
into body's movements. Seduced and
refined, the deer wish to have a taste
of which I am drinking, as they loose
themselves in my captivation. Crystal
diamonds of dew etched over the
treetops, tears of the night before,
nature's release on the velvet of the
petals, waking to first breath of
morning's light.

I am a diamond in the rough,
pure and unspoiled, perfectly intact
beneath a shroud of untamed foliage.
My sneakers are opening the door today,
as if entering life for the very first
time. Life having its own rhythm built
with glass, reflecting all past and
present, transposing reflective light
on the future as my sneakers balance
on the beauty of the myriad of stained
glass, each color pattern defines a
period of grace.

My sneakers speeding up my learning
curve, pointing me in forward direction,

glass all the way around, and, oddly
enough, pure silence...

Cohabiting effortlessly with nature,
connecting myself to misty tones of
pearl gray. Poetry of life, as I know all
too well, often births from unusual
places, translating life's beauty into
words of relevance, incorporating my
own sense of weights and pulleys,
which allow me to reposition my every
direction. The calmness of the morning
air corresponds as a sleeping giant about
to wake up. Broadening intensity begins
to mellow to a pale green shade of a
bird bearing poetic offerings, a cluster
of delicate flowers, each made of snow-
white porcelain.

Atop a tree, a solemn bird in a
lace collared red suit. Life, yet again,
reincarnated. What was once bold here is
now subtle, what was energetic now
calm, seemingly completely new, pushed
into different locations, amid muted

shades of pewter, silver and gray, as sky is transfigured, exotic thoughts thrown upon the gray linen wall, glinting with barely —there sunbeams shaded through. Seductive restraint, a departure from yesterday's full rays. The catalyst, something deeper driving the shifting of the gears, as Spring attempts to evolve to Summer, in the heating of the air.

My breath, intoxicated by the reincarnation, suggestive that I do not hold all the answers, the bird in red suit sits on my shoulder, promising not to cry. As the release of water from my pores collides with the morning air, I am not certain of the tear release from the bird. A wing, wipes away my indignities, revealing my grace on my brow. Dew falls like lemon drops, dying on the pavement, hastening the breath unfolding. A youthful rebellion ensues, as a pair of deer frolic on the hill. My breath unfolds in memories, sea feathers, floating weightlessly amid the slate of sky. My sneakers are my roots from which I grow, a predilection to solid grounding.

Fairy dust sprinkled in a hue of green, carried by the breeze, whispers of secrets yet untold, as my legs glisten under the veil of sweat, returning to the quiet enclave of distant dreams. Passions release, do I dare? Stepping into uncharted waters, hoisting my sail, I set out to sea. The paradox of the journey is in the following of the dream. My sneakers, my vessels now channeling me, as breath lends me courage in the silence I speak.

Sinuous curve of the sky is happily situated in the landscape, full of temples and palaces, all their sleekness and sophistication, the deer, content in the simplicity of their surroundings. The sky reminiscent of the ocean. Sea sponges blooming like bizarre flowers. With architectural silhouettes, and flamboyant colors, the flowers, and the morning air have a sculpture to them. Channeling the layered imagery of movement, emerging myself in thought, as sneakers lead the way. Life's architecture, all about the balance, breath fuses into a seamless entity, from a sublimely vaulted tomb to a marbled room of green meadows.

Beamed ceilings blossom with intricate painted flowers, whose delicacy speaks of soft roses. The air content in it's paving with what seems like acres of colorful mosaics, my ornate stepping-stones of passage. A sunlit gallery runs toward the river. With cypress carpet underfoot I take on the meadows ascent. My demure, hidden beyond a heavily fortified gate, shrouded in vines. Pale walls with subtle hints of mineral colors leading to emotion.

Life needs to be defined. Nature's compositions restrained and harmonious always evolving and adapting to the passage of time. Sense of serenity heightens the unfolding view, as a new day sparks a peaceful feeling. Wave rushes in, replenishing breath...

Idealistic longings, poetry becomes my watercolors, a kind of diamond that ravishes and flatters the eye independently of any subject matter or accuracy of metaphoric imitation. Sharply illuminated by an early sun against a mid blue sky. Streets are plunged in darkness, in a shifting, almost willful moodiness, as the trees sway in the strong of the wind. Here it is, I am at the moment when the sun rises hesitantly from beyond the trees, over the partially clad ground and sundry bark of the trees, as flower petals still seem partially asleep. Recalling memory in rich tones. So beguiling is the serenity of the air, that one might be surprised to learn that it depicts the very place, where, years earlier my soul drowned. Perhaps my family's suffering was the chaos I made order from in impeccably controlled poetry.

In my sneakers, I found life's emptiness could be suspended, if only for a time, in a perfect structure of

balance and compass, it was then that
I achieved in the devastating uncertainty,
a measure of peace. Grace falling like
raindrops on my fingertips, as I wipe away
the sweat from my brow, the suspended
drops now inching down my belly, soaking
my shirt. Questions from the wind, as
answers unwind, why me, why I?

As the Red Robin approaches,
eyewitness to my need. More intimately
scaled thoughts. Rare memories of a
similar age but widely different origins
arrive on first breath, in a familiar
location and space. I settle happily in
my sneakers. Deer, oddly performing a
naked dance. A number of misadventures,
even a few missed birds on the rocky road
to life's recovery.

Velvet, floral fabrics, and certainly
lace, all clothe my thoughts this
morning. The flower's fabric, indigo
blue and a fairly radiant yellow, are
strong enough to stand up against
the powerfully designed ribbon of sky.
Aesthetically driven, poetically literate,
serene, eccentric and wonderful, is the
air on my face. I carry within me a vivid
visual memory of what I remember.

Everything I see remains deeply imprinted upon my mind. The taste of my own breath, only a runner truly knows the exuberance in that momentary high, as my breath floats amid the air, as sneakers indulge me. The ligament in my calf is outreached in form, as I exhale up the hill. Encouragement comes from the extended hand of the Red Robin, as he whispers to my need. Fly away, fly away... and there I will...

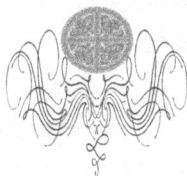

The birds, as they fly overhead, parade with elephant ears toward me, grabbing hold of whispers in the breeze, as if chosen secrets needing to be cherished. Crumpled flowers unfurl in a swirl of color, purple to velvety reds, as pink icicles erupt skyward. Profuse and fearless, deer surround, the green of the grass highlighting the abstract nature of their form. Rain governs the landscape of the day, and the configuration of life as a whole. Harmony in thought and color presents the manifesto that integrates my breath, as a hidden work of art. My sneakers are tangible accomplishments of imagination, tempering everyday existence with beauty and personal expression.

Always surrounding myself with what stimulates my senses, I am one whom aesthetics and life intertwine, as the practicalities of my life unfold. Loaded with fluctuations of tone and color, my run moves easily between mediums. My words, in their richness and hues, are my chosen paint for the day. Working fluidity and intuitively, veering from preliminary drafts and revising compositions as they evolve. Use of fragmented thought and sensuous color, brings breath and a continuity to my journey. Looking with eyes that see what was, as well as what isn't. I allow time and circumstance to create a harmony within my sneakers.

My brick walls, an architectural reaction to the fear that once seized me, as I crown the walls with broken glass to deter intruders. My walls, now, are slowly breaking down. Raindrops dancing amongst the pavement, as I ask

for a teacup from god to quench my
thirst. The tulip petal is falling from
grace, thus climbing back up. Percussion
of feet, percussion of breath, percussion
of heart... as I join in the rain's parade.
My teacup now holding a glass raindrop,
I quench my thirst.

Secrets sit silent in the darkest
place of memory, bursting as a star
against the dark of night I walk through
myself, to morning's light. Words are
eternal, transmitting experience into
living life. My breath begins to dance,
like a cork removed from a wine bottle
against the morning air. Passions run
fierce, frozen in time, my legs today, a
masterful sense of movement. Yielding a
host of questions and contradictions.
Psychological perspective of how I read
myself moving through life, and how I
read others moving through it, building
templates of thickly outlined patterns
and textures.

Life is blooming, and not just from the botanical view, the air of rebirth is unmistakable, immersing self with my sneakers. Just enough adequate heat and blue sky lends a generous dose of enchantment to me. A bird studies the bone structure of my face, perhaps, peering a view of my character. My breath imbued with mystery, a portal to somewhere else. Blending seamlessly with the air, my flesh collects specks of sweat to add to the collection. Rough wood ceiling, deliberately chipped floored tiles, nature's imperfections, slightly off, I like it.

The play of textures giving the air a sense of calm, and an unmistakable sensuality, having a transporting quality all of it's own, my breath seems consecrated by era rather than deep inhales and exhalations. Seizing the opportunity to redress a classic life, even keeping the drawbacks a part of the dark interior spaces, building a narrative around all of my existing components. I drop out of view, gently terracing down toward the river. Two wings clad in the gray blue stucco sky extend in opposite directions, sited by the river and the linear of my legs leading down the road. Water is glimmering, as the sun pours in from its skylight. My sneakers today, appropriately orientated. My glass walls turning my breath into a play of light and shadow, an almost cinematic image of calm, in my sneakers, full of serene.

One of my favorite places to be is few of tree limbs, then nothing but the water. My walls are lined with subtle shades of linen, my words painted to mimic marble, as my breath speaks the primary story. For me, the whole experience of life is the simple turning of a corner. The sun, so organic falling from my ceiling, somewhat breathlessly I bath in the view.

My asymmetrical facade and weather-looking shutters, become my nucleus conjoining present and past... my breath, simply paint on a canvas, as a treasured poem.

I gaze off into the distance before snapping back into the moment, and the unpretentious atmosphere of the morning. A black shadow glides past me in my peripheral vision. I turn in time to see the strength of the blackbird, as he sternly expands his wings. The imbalance of nature's distinctive tilt, as I too, am just a little to the left and off key. Beneath the stone and pavement I am lost in thought embedded in successive layers of mud. My peerless portfolio of alluring landscape imparting a sense of well being, as we all, are a sum of our parts. Soon happily replete, I blow away the cobwebs of yesteryear, the breeze minimal but delicious on my shoulders. It is an instant balm for my soul. Beginning to nod off to my breath's serene bobbing, my drifting senses are re awoken with some force at the suggestion of a breaking sweat developing down my legs.

Day is sinking against a total unoccupied season of thought. As my feet navigate the narrow street I wonder how my own experiences will compare after I resign from this earth. My pondering is answered by a clatter of shutters above my head. Looking up I am greeted by my host, tumultuously perched on the side of the tree, his ear to ear smile completed with a casual pecking of the trunk. Red beak evidently part of the fabric of the tree, as the pecking ensues. The woodpecker is a casual performer, as if the academic of his pecking is going to unravel some ancient mystery.

The deer, in their element, standing motionless, smiling, slightly amused at me not having found a better way of communicating, as sweat puddles around my navel. Contours of the hills are a fascinating shape, a life in profile, from the vantage point of my sneakers. The birds reciting a romantic tragic tale, setting me on my way, gazing as I drift from sight, my thoughts, sleeping and peaceful under the bird's tranquil spell. The journey ahead can't temper the feeling of calm that this morning's run and effortless pace of life has instilled in me. Determined to hold onto the feeling as long as I can back in the real world, resting assured that my breath will transport me back to gently lapping shores where the sea meets the sand.

Drifting in on the wings of birds and butterflies having buried my time capsule in the sand. My message in the bottle... sometimes the "dust" gets too complicated, as I wipe away the cobwebs, to see the gracious and timeless beauty in the rose, never revealing it's whole beauty on first glance... my sneakers, as well, never revealing my whole journey, nor answering the inquisitiveness of my first and last breath.

Moved by how light falls on a flower, and how the shadowing changes as the sun moves across the sky, as the morning air unfolds around me. Fearless, I run, dismantling walls between inner and outer self, the thrill is envisioning what still can be. A sharp compressed arrow straight to the heart, as the ray of sun hits my chest, vanishing I become part of the landscape. Picture frame images stand up, so much slipped away, before I could even say goodbye, silvery moon now overshadowed by the breaking of the sun. No farewell was left, as nighttime eclipsed to day. The northern star now in a solitary sleep, as my sneakers break over the hill. The trees great thirst, having been satisfied from last week's rain, foliage now an island of green height, light and space. Each leaf extending it's olive branch to me, reaching out to wipe the sweat from my shoulders. I am one with my clothes, as they rapidly adhere to my flesh, as my sweat becomes the adhesive. Seduced by air, my body submissive under the request of my breath.

Provocative, infectious passion of color, as my canvas is free, and paintbrush begins a self portrait. I am stripped from antiquated inhibitions, so much more becomes so much less. Flowers are reaching out in secret love affair, as yellow and purple caress each other in sacred places in the breeze. My sneakers are mindful of the privacy, avoiding all intrusion.

Shedding my skin, wanting to run

barefoot through the bed of tulips,
as their nakedness magnifies their
sensuality in a world we cover in cloth,
as a means to hide our own fears.
Nature is naked, and the simplicity of
that thought is so understated.

Flawlessness in the fluidity of
just being...

As I skim the surface, sometimes
it is the safest place to be. Deep in
the rhythm of my heart is where I pluck
a round of arrows out of the target.
The last rays of moonlight entering my
window, thoughts now stacked on a shelf.
Brushing my sneaker along the edge of
a tree, hoping to dislodge any glass
fragments that might have stuck. An odd
part of my brain now dismantled. The
adrenaline reservoir pours out, and floods
my body. Running so hard, that breath
pools at the corners of my mouth, as
my body explodes with electricity.

Streamlining myself, like a jaguar or

a leopard in the final moments of running downhill. Lying in the dim light that has layered out from the morning sky. An arrow embedded in my heart, as I grab with both hands, and pull it out... leaving droplets of blood along the pavement. No longer thundering, now I walk with soft steps, with the wind at my back...

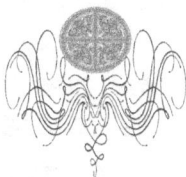

Today, I think I will fly. I will soar higher than the birds, beyond the clouds and the sun. I will drift through formations, as I float, looking down on all the mice and men. I will see god's creatures in minuscule scale, as my repertoire is painted in hues of violets and pinks. My thoughts will turn to sculpture in the sky, as granite and stone. The blood in my veins, my circulatory paths back to my heart, as drops of my rain fall upon earth. I will imagine a past life, as I leave dreams behind the now sleeping moon. I will run barefoot over the brick sidewalk of the sun, as the soles of my feet penetrate the heat. I will relax on a pillow of cloud, and drink wine with god. I will talk of condolences and offering of prayers, as he speaks of the golden wings of angels. Our eyes will meet, in a moment of truth, as my sneaker gets caught on the crest of the moon. I will breath in deeply, as I float above the Mediterranean Sea, finally landing on talcum soft pearl – peach sand, lying in complete stillness. I will lie forever in the crest of a wave, as the beat of my heart leaves imprints on the sand.

A power of embodiment plays across the sky. Wondering if we are all not just a painting of every moment of our existence. A song plays in the rhythm of my heart, as my feet eagerly dance along to the beat. Sun gods traveling my journey, washing down on me, as cleverly I drift out to my island in the sea.

Floating on a raft of my own breath, muscles twitch, as my pulse thunders in my ears. The clattering of butterflies propelling my shoulders, as the cords of my blood send flesh into euphoria. Running with the wind... a bluebird ties up my laces.

Morning church bells heard distant in the morning air. A background harmony, is now being sung by a bird. My sneakers, in the essence of their experience, pace to the resounding beat. Ducting under a tree limb, as a leaf grazes my shoulder, in the softest of poetic touch. The ensemble of the flowerbeds with throats reaching, pay homage to the sun. My breath drips onto tongues exposed, as petunias fight for the smallest of my quenching.

The flesh of my body leaves this place, drifting on sexual rhapsody, as each muscle twists in sensual healing against the heat of the open sky. Floating in a special time and place, my feet suspend mid air, hurdling over every thought that ever protruded from my soul. My heart muscle beating so loudly it reaches the mountains, sending ripples across the river. Whispering in the breeze, I close my eyes to the color of a dream, stillness wrapped in purples and violets, purity of air in a sinful blue, breath as pure as a dove, lies before me in linen white, my hand reaches up and captures the vapor.

Sending kisses outward to whomever formed the brilliance of the sun... as sun kissed shoulders wipe the sweat from my cheek, and I loose myself in my sneakers...

Delusions surround in the haze of the sun, shadowing my silhouette into an illusion, breath not spoken, whispers now heard, in the silence of the comfort of the trees. I slide inside my envelope of thought, pacing with the resounding flutter of the butterfly. All awake, yet

I still sleep in the stillness of my opened breath. Mirrored moon holding the point of nighttime dreams. I left behind. Tinge on my tongue tasting the salt of my own body, as the rhapsody of dance floats my legs into an eternal bliss.

Shrouded in fog, life hangs in suspension, within the boundaries of the trees. Absence of air, forgiveness of sin, breath eludes me into stillness. Requirement of thirst, as I quench on the dripping water laden foliage, now seeping down on me, as an early morning summer's shower. The deafening sound of silence, perfect stillness, no thought, no fear, no movement, as the woods hold all eternal secrets.

Red Robin in prayer, perched on a limb, I fold my hands in a compliance gesture. As feet intrude the earth, breath pulls at the heavens. Opening of chest, against a slate sky, as the amber of the sun, for today, is forgotten. I run in anticipation of tomorrow, out of this shroud of darkness, with the melancholic beating of my heart, my only recognizable sound. My sneaker's whispers, defy the pavement...

Iron curtain of fog suspends around each labored breath. Foliage covered in morning's dew, now drips of last night's torrent rain. Grey slate leaning of the ominous apocalypse just above the horizon. Mosquitoes quenching their need on the warmth of my flesh, drinking from my pores, as my feathered whisks can't deter them. My flesh now saturated, my clothes drenched, as I am suspended in my own body's dew. Heaviness of the current of air, as my body now slices through.

Battered tree limbs of last night's storms lie in corpse around me. My fingers run trails across my forehead, beads of sweat slope towards my nose. Cords of life suddenly release me, tilting back my head, inhaling through nose, sealing my lips, then release of air, my chest, now rising and falling, soothing my accumulated layers, the heel of my foot meeting no resistance with the pavement. Just beyond reach, no further messages coming from my brain, I expel in the heat... breathing in, breathing out, breathe fades to the pavement...

I am asleep in a field, my sneakers can't wake, my recovery place. Content in the changes of the morning, carrying out the final disposal of nighttime dreams. Every brush against the rose bush leaves me bleeding, as the brilliance of the sunlight blinds my every thought. Breath caught on a fragrant petal, as I linger on the scent...

Dewdrops are fading behind the fairy tale of morning sky. Dewdrop points leaking from treetops, as foliage fans my shoulders. Collapsing in the sheen of the river off in the distance, thoughts flying with the birds. Feeling the coolest of air against the tightest of breath, as my chest rises and falls with each labor of movement. Letting go, holding on, as I crash in the softness of breath, subdued and bewildered, riding the wave... somewhere where once I began and forever I have fallen.

Right now there is complete stillness. The winds wanting to carry me to the right, as my sneakers say left. Every leg muscle knowing its job, pulling and releasing me into breathe. Sandy gravel pushes me off with each step as I hit the paved road. Tilting my head back, arms pumping, expelling more breath, now riding on the wave of the wind. A new set of eyes on an old landscape, as the amber ball rises in the sky. Nighttime now faded, as flowers unfold, cool kiss of morning lingering on my exposed shoulders. Enjoying dabbling of shade that fringes the air, my own sea salt spray coating my tongue, as I take the curve on a drunken embrace.

My lullaby is swaying in the trees cocooned in my circle of color, adding earth tone hues to my tapestry. I am finger painting across the sky with my breath, happily replete in my early morning shrine. Landing at my door, I kick off my sneakers, and breath in the moment with delicate delight. SSSHHHH, as the whole world sleeps in slumber, my sneakers and I awake at dawn.

In the dead of the wood, my sneakers freeze, standing isolated in complete stillness, allowing my senses to lead me. The locomotion of the train faint in the distance, singing lullabies of the sparrows, trickling of a small, but

steady stream cascading over scattered
rocks, foliage etched through thin slices
of air in the slightest of breeze. The
curvature of a winding trail I have run
a thousand times before, in another
life, wild roses framing my form.
Gulping down life in vast quantities,
as I rise and fall through stages of
exhaustion, the dark mask of the woods
momentarily lifting, as beams of honey
stream through the tree tops. Cool
air rushes beneath, freshening the flesh
of my cheeks, evaporating the slope
of sweat on the bridge of my nose.
Running weightlessly, blinded by the
complete shadowy darkness under a
canopy of trees.

Adrenaline feeds in a fury throughout
my body, as the cords of my breath
release me. Believing we all shed our
bodies, as the essential "us" continues
in full rapid momentum, piercing my
skin into the abandoned quarry of my
empty stomach. Exhalation of stale
air, as tongue guides each bead of sweat,
delivering it to the passage of my
throat. A contemptuous look from some
sidelined deer firmly planted as a tree.

A cascade of air delivering the solitude of the pleasure I am seeking...

Struck by the absolute singularity of my pursuit, I become a laser beam, running up the hill into brilliant sunlight that makes me shade my eyes. Feeling the stab of every pebble beneath my feet, every twitch in the petal of the rose bush, as if the day has been torn apart and left in it's own bleeding. Deep breathing jerks my body into a salty sweetness, a momentary cure as my tendons spring loose. As the view of the water kidnaps me from daily life, my own sweat smells differently, the chemistry of my body altered, as sunlight pierces through the morning fog. My feet dancing in a dream, aching on the pavement, as my muscles contract and spasms are felt in the tingling of my toes.

Appearing in the earliest morning hours, where most pretenses fall away, rattled in my ill fitted windows,

noting that I have not always been so
psychologically touched by life. My body
rearranges itself, as I float on a pillow
of air, fingers run trails across my flesh,
as beads of sweat flake upon touch.
For the moment, primed by my morning
ritual, as I allow myself to drift,
sneakers taking over the kinetic memory
of my body.

The times of not hitting my target,
all the failures, having been fully felt,
again and again to get just even one of
these moments of flow. Left abandoned
and naked without my loin cloth, in
front of a clothed world... I run home.

My chest and belly fill with air. On
the release of breath, I open my sprint
with hydraulic fluidity. My shoulders are
back and down. I look like a tree trunk
swaying with imperceptible movement,
and then I enter my point of stillness.
Tiny muscles around my lips struggle to
whisk back droplets of heavy sweat.

Anchored to the ground, showing what little impact an impending world can have on me, with a force that has welled up from my dank, unused places. Hand at my waist, inching upward, I am connecting with a set of newly exposed ribs, declining my shirt. Dreams are laden, as I find a wisp of them, an echo, a feather touch, of what I have discovered beneath my waves, and why I hope life ends on a beach, with my feet submerged in pearl peach sand, and the view of the sea is what my eyes come to finally rest upon. At low tide, miles of beach revealed, tide comes in, waves are huge and crash against the breakwater. The swell of waves, the ragged outline of submerged rocks and the dramatic silhouette of islands, captures the essence of my exposed dream.

Drops of sweat fall around me like flower petals, as my skin unzips caught in the rake of the sun's light, my feet penetrate the earth.

Blinking in the bright relentless sunlight, as the over ripe mango sits high in the sky. In the opening between breaths, the world has grown larger. The world now clear as glass, thoughts now crystallize. Lancing a gigantic wound, years of poison released through my sweat glands, as the liquid shatters on the heat of the brick sidewalk. The core of my weathered frame tucked behind a facade, on either side with limited regard for symmetry. No other eyes have scanned my thoughts, my flesh so hot it flushes my skin the color of azaleas.

Picking up my feet in an all-encompassing whirring, as the effect of the intoxication rushes ahead of my shadow. Entranced in deep philosophical thought on a full sun rising. A good life, a very good life, is finding one person who knows you, who shares the joy in your pleasures, of running damp and happy in the heavy dew of morning, of sitting with you while you ramble with abandon.

Feeling the unstoppable convulsion of my heart, the pulsating of my own blood through my veins, a languishing river drips down the curve of ligaments in my legs.

Open eyed, I breath in, in total full bodied contentment... breathing out on a gilded prayer, as sun tattoos penetrate my flesh in a deep embrace.

My upper body tilted back in euphoria, as my eyes squeeze shut in crinkled joy. Legs extended under the folds of heat, covered in body dew, undetected by my flickering nostrils; as droplets collide undisturbed beneath my breath. The flagpole settles to a steady sway from a quiet breeze. Each round molecule of my scent rolling off my upper lip with urgent desire, driving into my bloodstream, taking an express to my brain. My body responding in a jet stream of warmth cascading between my eyes, and spiraling with enormous speed through my ribs, pooling between my legs, gaining speed in flourishing agony down the inside of my thighs, finally letting out the tips of my toes.

Feeling my heart beat steady on

command, noting the calmness of the release. I step closer to the edge with each breath, suddenly putting my hands out on the edge of my jaw, I whisk droplets into the air, edging ever closer to my reflection pool. Discovering the life altering revelation that joy can exist in unexpected forgotten places, as I am falling with the sun, drowning in it's light...

Having completed my soaking under the stars, waking from the restorative, nurturing elixir I call sleep, I emerge as scattered clouds mosey across a powder blue sky. Humidity so thick and hot it flushes my skin the color of azaleas the moment I step into it. Water drops evaporating in the sunshine, I stand in magnificent and improbable isolation; serene and commanding on a calm day.

Sparrows circle each other in tandem, as I float on my back, ears below the surface, as the world falls almost completely silent. Seduced in the paradisiacal notion of my unself-conscious poetry with that extra little frolic of glee that comes from being completely naked. A spontaneous strip, no pause to slumber as I release into a dramatic silhouette of breath...

My trail winds along the edge of the park, listening for tree frogs in the rain forest canopy up above, watching for flashes of color, as red robins and green crested hummingbirds, take to flight. Trying to imitate their moves, I am awed by their energy. I am ready to prostrate myself and beg them to accept me as a student. In a shining light of compassion and understanding in the hummingbird's eyes, as if to say "You are too much in a hurry" he states. He might just be referring to my life. "Wisdom requires patience." Melodious music wafts from somewhere. On the spur of the moment, I stop. Grass is my yoga mat. I bend and execute a perfect head to toe extension, years of practice have not left me. As the birds clap, I get back up on my feet, wave at my feathered friends, turn, and head for the hill for the long climb home.

Somewhere between beginning and end I step into a bout of aromatic sweating, and I drink from its young wine. Each breath drawing in a smoky bouquet. Feeling the tingle in my steam, as though the scent were brushing up against my cheeks. On my outside, steam billows off my naked body, as I channel the forest. Sailing into a billowing whiteness of mini eternity...

The beginning of a beautiful weekend of sunshine, soft sand, translucent waters, a place to just arrive and to pause. Melding into a harmonious whole can be much more complicated than just knocking down a wall, as everything that happens to us becomes carved into our

wood. As I trundle along, I find myself
tucked between strands of brush.
Definitely private, a little hedonistic
even, the day unfolds before me. Utterly
untouched air, offering the solitude I
crave. I am standing waist deep in water,
inspecting the drenching of my toes, as
the coating of salt coats down my legs.
My sneakers allow me to explore, detail
the route to the unmarked road that
leads me here and there, fortuitously
allowing me to explore.

Wet dew brushes my legs, and last
night's spider webs span the trail. I
detour through a tangle of vines. The
purr of air beckons in the distance, a
hole in the foliage teases with a glimpse
of honey amber rays, as my sails
punctuate the horizon. I am completely,
blissfully alone. I stop, riveted to the
spot, as in and out, I breathe!

Straining up the hill, I turn right
into the park, why, always amuses me,

as never a fan of insects, the scorching
heat has them more pronounced than
usual in the humidity of air. It is the
eclipsing of foliage, as much as the
serenity of the calm, I think, that
pulls me to a wooded trail, as the
toxins from my soul empty and the
gnats and mosquitoes drink from the
deluge of my impurities. The curve of my
path, now lingering at the tip of my
nose, as the scent of wild roses, nature's
natural seeding, fills my breath, the
crisp white of their flowering is simple
beauty. The steam bath of morning heat
deeply penetrates the small white
clusters, as the simplicity of their
fragrance becomes the empowerment of
morning's air.

In equal pace of breath and feet, I
breathe, as the drenching of my cloth
floats me on a dream. The rose weighs
heavy on breath, lingering, I pause in
the foliage, as unobtrusive liquid
sunshine pours down, I indulge on it's
hot sauce, closing my eyes letting
myself hear, smell, taste and touch,
allowing raspberry crystals to pour from
my forehead... heat is my friend, as the

temperature rises, and I am alone in my sauna.

Not from where I began, where I am, or what I am to become, as life lies still as a picture before me, as I wondrously blink in the sunlight, I am morphed in the grace of just letting life unfold for me. Metaphysically I am broken down, as subtle threads of currents run along my flesh, reminding me, once again, that I too, am just human. So it is that I find myself tramping down a shady woodland path, my breath as a warm blue sea I splash around in. Warm sunshine tempered by the slightest breeze, as I stride out along a dry and dusty footpath between which the sea glitters and my breath flashes across the blue-green sky. I could stay in this exact spot for eternity, the mapping of heated sweat over the whole of me.

Life's illusions become reality, as I

embroider them across the ribbon of
Mediterranean blue just above my breath.
As the dissolution of two souls become
as one, and the spontaneity of life
unfolds before my eyes. As much as we
try to paint life, more times than not,
life paints for us, and the architecture
is more beautiful than we could have
ever hoped for. The cracked walls, the
flaws, the imperfections, all find a
way to turn into a breathtaking work
of art... all we can do is sit back and
watch, close our eyes in the mystery,
revel in the timeless grace of the
moment, and scarlet love letters.

Opening my embroidered silk blinds,
to yet, another day, threading roses
into garlands. Flowery, extravagant
detail, taking a prodigious amount of
forethought, sumptuously mirrored. A
composition of peacock blue hangs from
the ceiling, as night stars dissipate
behind the breaking of the sun. Verses of

poetic rhythm etched on my walls and trunk, as an olive gray blanket of fabric encloses me as I wander through the wood's foliage.

Running, a form of freedom, resisting any kind of organization, I am out here on my own, an adventurer in another world. Carried away by momentum, arduous exertion, symbiotic force, to the edge of the world. Bumbling in and out, intermittently flipping through photographs of my life, carrying me, my sneakers dual as my confidante, as the river becomes a mystical sign, I now run to. The curved shape of oasis borrowing pleasing views of the trees, I mingle easily. Picking out thoughts from my massive stone retreat, as heat radiates through my body. Wrapped in the self – protection of silence, as breath vapors escape into the air.

I am neither here, nor there rather just floating above in timeless suspension. Over all the rocks that I have tripped, stumbled and fallen, today my path is clear, as I navigate the world, and thirst on a moment's breath for even more... as my sneakers begin their ascent...

At night's closure, I find peace and serenity under the observation of the sun. The point on the hill revealing full view the river's depths, as the mountains echo the force of my human spirit in it's unrestricted solitude. Drops of sweat lay as diamonds on my chest, I lavish in the timelessness of the gems. A diamond in the rough, as the sun is blinding against my clarity.

As breath bequeaths the diamonds, the treasures cascade down my flesh, breaking upon the pavement. The crystal reflection pool at my feet honoring the silhouette of my shadow. Rainbow reflection of water colors, as pink and purple hues become the color pattern of breath. Sun gods seduce my flesh, setting fire to movement of my body.

The echo of the mountains deafening in their sound of silence, allowing thoughts to collide in their backdrop, in a thunderous roar my thoughts now carry me. Floating over the river, heaven bound, as diamonds drop into the water below, not shattering the prism of color. In their rainbow I am caught on a crashing symphony of breath. The echo becomes the music of my pulsating heart, resonating across the sheen of river. I too, resonate, in the dripping stream of diamonds.

A seagull admiring the stream now cascading down my naked flesh, quenches his thirst at the river's edge, untouched by the absence of world around him, as morning unveils itself to the sun god now encroaching above... I drift on a sheet of air...

My solitary sail flutters in the breeze, as the pale blues and silver grays of the sea merge with the rose gold of the uploading sun. As everywhere you look, my walls are adorned with my serene feminine canvasses, as my hues of pink turn to gold upon my running into an embrace with the sun. Hypnotic effect of passing clouds caught in my glass skylight, poetic imagery, my most evocative shrine, a balmy, Bohemian enclave of thought, where breathtaking sea views and pearl granular sand await me. Following sound into silence, I listen for the sea. Positioning myself carefully in the sun as a bead of sweat is flicked away by my reflection, cascading along the pavement.

Blooms burst from a bucket of roadside flowers, organ music of the bird's sounds faintly in the distance. My heart arranged over concentric semicircles of breath, along a cobblestone pathway. My breath crisscrosses over smaller pathways, collected icicle tears hang as spider webs frozen in time. The stream of my pulse and my breath, meet as two rivers, swirling impromptu, a sudden impulse as I run along, without calculation or fear. The solicitude of air preventing the impinging of reality, caught in imagination, in another world, that is for me, a small paradise.

Surreptitiously my eyes yearn after me, as the scent of my unaltered sweat now bathed in salt, lingers on the tip of my nose, proving a powerful restorative in the cool of the morning air.

Painting my portrait across open sky, as Van Gogh holds my brush in hand. Painting the trees the color of tulips, the sky the color of the trees, watering the flowers with icicle tears left on the pavement in the heat. Feeling the need to break from breath, my legs unfurl in pace as I run toward the river. The crystalline of the sun on the breaking of day, as the toxins of poison are released in my sweat, coursing through my veins, the vessel of my choosing. I am enveloped in scattered thoughts on the heat of a summer's day, as a deer waves me on, and in a nodding glance, I heed.

Drama unfolds under the sun, where moon beams once held, walking to the edge of the shore, I swirl my hands and feet in the sea. Conditions

are right, and the water sparkles. White
puffs allude as a brilliant orange beak
unfolds above in the horizon. Millions
of unspoiled thoughts float around
me in dark green water, like stars in
my miniature galaxy. Thoughts follow
the sun on their daily migration, my
venomous defenses picking and choosing
what ones stay, what ones I leave
by the wayside. I float through the
glowing stars. Feeling the soft tickle
of heated bubbles percolating out of
my shoulders. All around me, circles
of silver bubbles rise, a relief valve
of sorts for the densest concentration
of my pores.

Starring into the sun, sorting
pearls, arranging by color, rearranging
by size, each drop of sweat sorted
to a dream. Pearls glisten under the
light of day. Pearls, defined by their
beauty, capturing mental photographs,
intimate emotions, patterns, scale
and poignancy that all converge to create
my natural wonders. The deeper I have
been willing to delve on foot, the
more I have revealed to me. At the
beginning of the day all my external

stories are simply containers for my inner narrative.

Finding a place where I feel free, other places I know my perception is distorted and my actions afflicted. The air blessedly cooler today, defined by constant change and a sense of formal eternity. My breath reveals, then covers up, then sighs heavily as my run climaxes on the crest of the hill. Gingerly rolling up cloth, exposing flesh of my mid body, coolest air evaporating the pearl beads of sweat. Breath catches on a breeze, as I close my eyes, drifting into an altered state of consciousness, as a custom balanced formula is extracted from the flowers.

So massive are my pillars, and other fragments that remain, the fantastical scale of my ruins, still stained with soot, profoundly imperfect as any unscripted human life can be. Trees, as Spanish moss, drape over me, shaking my kaleidoscope, as the world, now, turns vibrantly green... seducing me into a worry-free unreal reality, if even for just a short time, as my mind runs free...

I linger for a few moments in the spit of contented heat this morning, as a short run takes me through spruce woods onto the pavement. My brain buzzes with anticipation for the day, as I swat back drips of sweat from my brow. The first glimpse of sun through the trees blasts the chatter from my mind, as the long curve of road beckons my distance. A blackbird shrieks from the treetops, as the light over the hill becomes a golden hue, a chipmunk burrows onto my path.

Turning the same observant eye back to memory, inscribing a tangible character, me, into a story. Transforming thoughts into something darker and raw, bringing an immediate to a meditative run. Relying heavily on metaphors for perspective, heartbreakingly honest emergence back into life, after a journey of detours, and the haunting peace it sometimes ensues.

My breath is drenched in salt, as legs

clamor in the heaviness of the air,
remedying my thirst on salt beads,
looking up at the cooling mirage of blue
ocean skyward.

Eclipsing the sun as I climb up
over the crest of the hill, leaving my
breath at the river's edge as I pant the
heat's forgiveness...

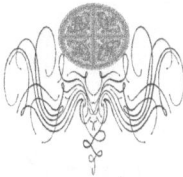

How do a thousand voices fall
upon me, from the darkest of night?
Daylight breaks, emerging from my
rubble – strewn interior, my weathered
silhouette graced by my loosely allusive
sneakers, flesh now in a palatable gloss.
Running along a casual scatter of old
marble fragments, sipping on glasses of
human toxin, my sneakers migration has
spanned a lifetime.

Harboring secret beaches, sights and
sounds, struggling through thunderous
waves towards the horizon with heart
yearning, feeling deficient, so ever use
to being alone. Breath escapes me as I

reach up a hand, an attempt to
recapture a lost vapor in the wind...
the pulsating of my own heart, the
only sound left in a solitary echo
against the flash of the morning sky...
a bird lands on my shoulder, expansion
of wing wipes away a tear.

Morning opens against the hush of
silent waves. Sneakers lay quiet in
delicate sprints along the boardwalk.
Sand pinching at my ankles, as sweat
drips in large currents down my back.
Seagulls pillage on yesterdays lunch,
shells take refuge in an early rising
tide. Looking towards the sea for
answers, I close my eyes in the breeze.
Forgotten dreams imprinted so close
to shore, it is hard to see where dry
sand ends.
A teardrop carried on the roll of a
wave, as eyes burn from salt spray of my
own dew. Colorless, odorless, thoughts
float out on a migrant sea... teardrops

rest on an oyster shell, breath lays silent, as the crash of a wave on shore, is the only noise I hear. I breathe in at the mystery of the sea!

My illusive kingdom by the sea, sun is out, morning landscape is blissfully quiet. Glancing at the long expanse of sandy beach beyond the houses, out for a run along the sand. Standing on my island of solitude, watching lights drift on a distant shore. In the spirit of a week of slow-lane lifestyle, thoughts cruise along with sea birds and dolphins. The sky is empty blue, as sand sweeps away to distant peaks. Life, in its purest, least tainted form, as waves crash along the shore, pebbles roll in the wake. The sea cascades over my sneakers, flesh washed by sea salt, as seaweed clings to my ankles. Coral sprouts from my pores in delicate pinks, as breath rolls in rhythm with the tide.

Morning dew drapes from all body parts, as my silhouette takes rest in open water. Breath now sun kissed...

Flesh drips in honey, as breath channels into the sea, gently caressing a beach lapped by the bluest morning breeze. Seaweed refreshing my skin, as sea salt spray takes care of the quenching. Shadows fall ahead, as seagulls take shape tickling toes in waves, hermit crabs cross my path. Enveloped in the calm of the sea, body dew lewdly dripping from all points of flesh.

Kicking off sneakers, dropping shorts in a pool beneath my feet, body spirals downward, in a skinny dip release of a heated run, all flesh surrenders to the bareness of a cool morning air... as air moves through vibrations on my nakedness, parting ripples in the water. Heartbeat resounds in the silence of my voice...

Looking unflinchingly at the sea, erogenous in every wave swept breath. Broken, cracked, smelling of sea salt, as jagged lighting bolts penetrate the sky, my legs contract, bringing my body to a standing. Feeling the steady caffeine – driven thump of my heart. A brief moment of red before the sun settles in its daily dress of yellow, and I settle into my daily deluge of jolts through my legs, as if bones were dislodging from my hips.

Sympathy flickers across the sky, as if I am standing naked in a life that's happening too fast: slowing down my accelerator, blood pumps coarsely, as sneakers fall back into last nights dreams. Sneakers navigating around phobias and nightmares, enough to tolerate the precipitous drop of momentarily despair, long enough to find my way out again.

Shadow runs ahead in perfect tune with the universe, as my heart pulsates

hard, just to keep up. Warm under the
heated sun, cool sea breeze on my face,
my vision of body like Michelangelo's,
sketches across a naked sea of sky.
My hands are starfish, imprinted on
a portrait of peach sand, as breath
uncovers from, yet, another unfolding...

Waves break along the shore, as sand
fills my sneakers. Sand angels left
basking in the dawn. Cascading rays
of sun touch down on talcum soft
iridescent granules, as hermit crabs
rush to my racing. Breath ensconced in
a morning cocktail, as toxic drips of
humidity taste upon my lips. A conduit
of flesh for the river of my pores opens,
as waterways. Circle around my navel.
Breath escapes me, as eyelashes flicker
on the newest of rays over the horizon.
Eyes rest on the meditation of rippled
water, as sea horses bob in the distance.
Soul is still, as I breathe in the salted
morning air...

In the hurried of the morning's heat, my sneakers succumb to the force of nature. Waterfalls cascade from my brow, down the curvature of body parts, pooling in vibrations throughout my soul. Blood pumps furiously, in failed attempts at escaping the humidity, my tongue languishes on drops of salt. Thoughts suspend in the torching, as I drift in purple haze against illusions. Coral reefs and Mediterranean Sea breezes, in a mirage of my choosing. Anchored in the vision, sea horses ride my wave of breath.

Opening laces, illusions left on the sidewalk, paired with my sneakers, drowned by the quenching of a salt laden tide. Sun now rising, mirage falls silent, amid painted sky...

Ghosts swirl in the hollows of the heated hallways. Deadness of morning air has my flesh looking in both directions for a place of refuge. Almost instinctive now, my sneakers skip to the covering of shade beneath the dripping foliage. Drips dry before hitting the pavement, evaporating on flesh, as secrets long lost forgotten, erode with the scorching. The scolding of the heat, punishment for laughing at the cold winds of winter.

Heavy hands of ghosts suspend above me, in an attempt to pull me back, my feet lunge forward. Lilac painted — silk walls and satin curtains drawn around my windows, shedding water droplets, in a retrieve of breath. The pavement now perfectly waxed, as the heat steals the illusion of any shadow. Refurbished and refreshed, is not going to come easy on the spill of Mother Nature today.

Lushness of early morning silence echoes from each rose petal. Succulent

beads of dew hang suspended above each
thorn. The scent of heat so thick it
latches onto my breath, my sneakers peer
out from a black frame of pavement.
Heat, as an antique paisley shawl, wrapped
so tight, it cuts off my breath. Sweat
hanging as ornate costume jewelry around
my neck.

Presiding over recurring interactions
with the birds, with their sartorial
flair for creative expression, as they
nose dive in patterns across the sinuous
sky. Pretending nothing exists in pewter,
silver, and peacock - blue sky, layered
in gold leaf paper, knocking down my
walls. Purple haze scripts out breath
in crystallized sweat, as my tongue
languishes for a drop...

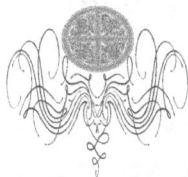

Sometimes wanting to do everything.
Run beyond every hill. Investigate every
bend in the road. Other times, simply
wanting to slow down, relax, as the sun
pampers my spirit. Enjoying the massage

of sunbeams on my shoulders. From the inside of my reflection pool, to the edge of the world, I unwind in naked seclusion, absent of fear.

Waiting for morning tides to rise above my sandbar, weaving through thought patterns, defined by constant change and a sense of eternity. My tide reveals, the feel of a never – never – land, watching the river flow...

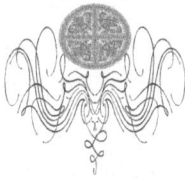

An ocean of turquoise blue carries my breath in flight with the birds. The peek – a –boo play of my shadow, melts ahead of me, spillage evaporating in the sizzle of the pavement. The sun light torch piercing my back, as a river runs deep down the curvature of my spine. Hands outstretched as starfish, catching whisks of my body's dew, as my eyelashes wash away the impurities from my eyes.

Gold and gray concrete facade of sky lulling me awake to changing colors, subliminal hums and whirs of passing

insects in flight. Drying myself on
a handkerchief of flesh, running
thunderously towards the horizon.
The deep body of black still air moves
against me. Propelled by some symbiotic
force as deer lazily graze in the shade.
Sea - fans waving gently, as I swim
across the sky.

Sea sponges sprout from my ears,
soaking up the residual dew of my body.
Draped in the coolness of seaweed, as
cucumber waters spill from my breath.
Gazing up at the timelessness of the
hill as a crystal chandelier of the sun,
exposes droplets entrapped in the
fountain of my pores. Path of droplets
on the fire of the pavement, as my
sneakers succumb to the scorching.
    Closing my eyes, I see the casein
image of the sea, as I strip down to
the poetry of my bareness, and submerge,
naked, into the cooling waters of the
harbor. I float as coral among the

deepening of the blues and greens, as I ponder in the deluge of pure sweat.

The smallest of rounded molecules rolling down my brow, out spoken from every body cavity across my flesh, painting a canvas across my belly. Stepping closer to the edge of pure delusion, under the direction of the forsaken relentless heat of the sun. The suns torch whipping at my shoulder blades, taking direct aim at my exposed flash. Lashes of heat carved out in a mural on my back, oranges and reds pulsating from my bloodstream.

Quickening of pulse, yanking me further from last night's dreams, knocking down my walls. My river waters translucent, air so hot it pricks at my skin, in darted motion. Melding into a whole, pausing for the change, leaving an orange glow in my wake, myself, following sound into silence... as I drop in the heat!

All efforts are thwarted, as if I am walking a path in the desert. Mirage of ocean opens up ahead, as I panic in my own intensity of body heat. Sun spilling down over me, air so thick, muscles twitch as they slice through the iron curtain of humidity. My body heat, melting the steel cage suspended around me, as a breath escapes in suspended vapors. A euphoric rush of adrenaline, feeds the frenzy of the salted river cascading down my breasts, filling my navel.

Illusion of water castles before my eyes as my eyelashes swim the breaststroke, as the panting of my lungs, labor in the stillness of dry air. The unforgiving fortitude of the heat...

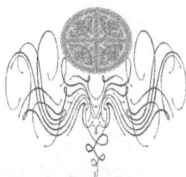

Splashes of heat radiate off of me, igniting colors of my tapestry, as a symphony of air passes above me.

Adorned jewelry of salt beads around my neck, heading East into the sprawling sun, my naked body revealed just beneath my loin cloth, as unbridled intimacy floats down the curvature of my belly. Navigating the area of my navel, sweat settles under deep emotion at the crest of my pelvis. The area between my hipbones opens wider in full sprint, ligaments molding with the motion. Tickle of air against my face, as religion is released across the sky, as the clay my breath now sculpts from.

In every sip of morning dew, gathered wisdom... as I enter "my place of peace, and self indulgence," trapped on the tip of my tongue, a solitary whisper in the wind...

The privileged window from which I wake, moonlit marble, and the various thoughts I had last night, all chisel out under the morning sun. Beneath the trees, I turn diamonds into a pattern of secrets. Only slowly, do I realize, from passing glimpses through half - open doors, that almost every pattern of diamond is different. Reflecting as prisms bouncing off the mountains to the edge of the world, my flesh is dipped in honey. I'm floating amid millimeters of tiny drops of salt laden water, unrecognizable texture to the diamonds. I'm throwing diamonds to the sun, as one or two bounce off my breath. Cascade of diamonds sparkle, casting a rainbow as they fall, I am falling too.

Subdued calmness. A golden wheat wall of color lies ahead in the majestic of the mountains, in my freewheeling downfall, my pace picks up. Indulgent, I clasp the diamond closest to me, as I melt in the shimmer of its glass, as my body's dew drips from my flesh. Looking at the world through the eye of a diamond, as my breath segues into the air.

The mere deceptions of the sun,
as the birds playact in suspended
flight, watching me with conspiratorial
glances. Careful balance constructed, as
I question the desire of overwhelming
heat. Offering of free advice from
the sun gods is spoken in innocents,
launching into a meditative cleansing,
feeling my body, blur with the watery
sounds, via my vessel of dripping
salted sweat.

The sun is now coming in low
and touching my arms. The air is hot
and thick, as my sneakers find their
light- footprint approach on the
melting on the pavement. Arcing in
unison just feet away, theatrically
posed deer in playful make- believe,
sauntering along gleefully. Drifting
into an altered state of consciousness,
allowing thoughts to collapse in an
unmistakable air of refinement and
romance.

Breath revels, covers up, and then,
sighs heavily, as humidity drapes me in
its Spanish moss. Waiting for my morning
tide to raise me above my sand bar... and
drift me out to sea.

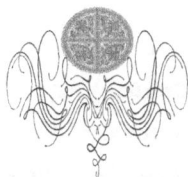

My solitary yacht sail flutters in the breeze, as the pale blue and silver grays of the sea merge with the rose gold of the sun. My feet amble back to my wooded retreat, hidden away under my canopy a thousand miles logged, under sometimes, a freezing rain and whistling wind.

Today, the cold is only a mirage, as the humidity dampens my breath on first clash with the morning's air. Staleness of heat lays as sticky honey on my flesh, as eyelashes cling to all of my impurities. The rose gold sun is now raised high off the mountains shadowing the river with its after-thoughts.

Belly rising and falling with each conquered breath, as lungs swell in anticipation of a greater exhale. Dew drips from my brow, lingering on my cheek, pondering the curve of my face...

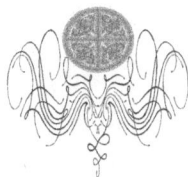

Stepping off the curb, running round the bend, toes touching, heels suspended. Dreams so laden with sweat that I could easily drown in my own pool of intoxication. Looking like a tree trunk swaying with imperceptible movement, it is then I enter stillness. I pantomime pulling back, anchored to the ground, my breath picks up, carrying messages in the wind. Curling up my shirt, exposing flesh, feeling naked in the heavy heat. Practicing finding center, dropping my energy down, pulling energy back up, breathing from my belly, letting all of my breath out, then the deeper stillness rides within me. The wave of current as a fire begins in my feet, filling my lungs until it overtakes my conscious, an unexpected nudge from my lungs as my torso shifts forward.

The decision is to drop my defenses, and the admission of my novice standing against the hollow of the open sky. Suddenly, the treetops begin to dance...

My feet are dancing across the page, escaping towards the sea. Hard not to be smitten, as I float disappearing into a sea of shells. Neither grand, nor pretentious, my blood the color of fine red wine bringing a sense of decadent to my breath. Hypnotic effect of a passing cloud stuns me.

The sun in a warm glamorous hue of pink turning into gold. Humming the sound of the sea, as it appeases my soul. Running along my cliffs, diving into the embrace, 'a place just to be,' as I need the solace from time to time. The sky has an undoubtedly welcoming, comfortable feel, as it splashes paint along my walls. Sometimes battered by storms, sometimes utterly tranquil...

The unabashed joy of direct caressing sunlight, I scream "touch me, touch me," as small flickers etch from behind the clouds. Exhaling stale air into the extinguishing momentary flow of the clouds. Recognizing today will have to be a contrived dream, on an endless beach on a golden summer's day, as thought far removes me from the thunderous sullen clouds overhead.

I slide my sneakers along the pavement, and speak in whispers to the birds, as they drink on the nectar of honeybees. Recoiled, I am swimming on a sea of breath, as jagged lighting bolts of humidity now rest on my shoulders. The controlled silence of the woods, as the pulsating of my blood circulates my veins.

Crisscrossing every trail along the beach, through dried beach grass, abandoning all hope of seeing the blood red sun peeking out from over the horizon. For today, I run before the rain, breath rising from the empty tangles of my center, merging in the path of wild roses, spirals of energy releasing me into a calm...

My senses shined up like silver, as verses etch across the sky. My nose fills with the scent of fresh cut grass, in a moment of redemption. Peering from my ocean of light to the wooded trail. Breath fills my lungs, wraps around my heart, escapes through the portal of my softened lips, leaving it's vapors as mist on my eyes. From beginning to end, my legs unfurl in the summer's heat. Delusions escape under the burning of my brow.

"I don't know who you are," the red robin whispers into my mirror, speaking close enough to leave a circle of fog on the etching of my glass. "Come fly with me and I'll tell you of truths yet spoken, as I serenade your breath into a complete darkness of sleep."

Sweat burns my eyes, as the encroachment of trees haunt of yesteryear. Violins play soundly in the backdrop, as names and places are remembered in the logging of my miles. Another time, another place, my sweat dribbled on distant lands, ravaged by my soul, forgotten by the mighty sword of fate, as wall sconces light my way in the darkness.

An early morning, not yet swept away by the shadow of the moon. My breath felt heavy in my chest, as feet press into the blackness of pavement. An early rising blue jay leads me to the honey glow of sunrise, as dew covered petals of crimson rose release their tongues in the flutter of my sweat. A whisper brushes across my eyelash, as the silent cries of carnage fill the bones of the forest, as last night's feast of animals leave some to carcass.

Paradox of life and death in the thunderous beating of my heart, as I ascend up the hill. My own carnage now left on the side of the road... forever remembering, another time, another place, where once I stood in the deadened silence of yesteryear.

Taking a larger breath, falling one step backward into the camouflage of the foliage. Faint sounds of an unfolding morning heard. My sculpture tilts back in a red robin's playing of a saxophone, breath expanded so fully that my walls are bending outward to contain it. Purposeful wondering, deer playing peek a boo tracing my footsteps. Allowing scent to outplay thought, a wild rose bush encroaches my path, lingering at the tip of my nose.

Each round molecule of sweat rolling off my upper lip with urgent desire, falling onto stone-lined garden spaces, as shoulders are pierced by the crimson heat of the sun. The arrows of each ray penetrating, as both hands grab hold of the arrows in a release of breath...

Raindrops turn to sun drops, as they melt like dew, on the tips of my eyelashes. Forecasting thoughts too deep to reveal, I skip along to the river's edge. Melting into the mountains, the water so much greater than I. Beads of perspiration fall like flower petals as the disparity holds the paradox of the day.

Leisurely delivering little spurts of effort, my breath falling through my body, tumbling down into my lungs. Running damp and happy in the heavy dew of morning. Tingles of freedom run up my spine, unimpeded from my tailbone to the top of my head. Allowing muscles and bones to take over, drifting on this new strange sensation. Breath, now fewer, straying to the outer edges...

Showering in the rain, as my shadow remains within the boundary of the drops. Stretching out through legs, feeling the suppleness extend up and through the curvature of my spine, creating the feeling of being bare and naked. Breathing deeply and evenly, riding each inhalation, moving body with a wavelike pulsation to a deeper release of rest. The air has once again, become smooth, as my sneakers pick up, my sails unfurl overhead, as the silvery streak of my silhouette fades in the foliage. Waiting on an inevitable thunderstorm for the rays to shine again.

Hydrotherapy has made me putty in the hands of the storm gods... as showery drops drench my flesh, I forget, from where once I began.

I pass through, holding my breath, feeling my heart beat steady at the command of my sneakers. A voice tells me, to take a breath, release a breath, and then to hold in the stillness. In the opening between breaths the world opens wider, clear as glass, as the wind blows tracing the lines of my face. The river in the distance changing course from north to south, as it cauterizes my lungs in the deepest of places.

A cord of connection, a braid of fuchsia and green, fragrant like wild

roses, as the river's ripples echo in the
rhythmic measure of my heart. I breath
into the echo, in an expanded release,
as the sun's rays etch into my forehead,
penetrating the faucet of my pores,
as drips begin to trickle down my
shoulders, it's crust of salt ripples
down the curvature of my belly, as flood
gates from my navel open up.

Pressing myself against a wall of
sky, exhaling stale air, the sun peering
directly through my skin. My body just
a costume for my play, as my sneakers
collide in a serendipity dance. Shells
of breath slaved out along the beach,
my muscles contract with each step.
The day's nectar fills the area between
my hipbones, as my joints and tendons
open up.

Air moving in and out of me, like
the passing of seasons, happily painting
at my easel, as thoughts collide into
color across the Mediterranean Sea of

sky. Sipping on the nectar of honeybees, drunk on my own intoxication... calming stillness of my breath deepens into my abdomen, as it escapes through my feet, drips from my pores now scattered along the pavement. Foliage fanning my flesh, as heat rises into a sensual heated explosion. Riding the wave of euphoria!

Sweat beads, in a constant flow, as my feet are unnervingly self - sufficient in the undertaking. Jig sawing up the terrain, rising out of the trees like a fortress. A burning that lifts only as I run again, feeling tiny pebbles on the pavement beneath my soles. The hill is my landscape of choice for the day. My sneakers don't complain about anything, as my spine surges forward from the anchor of my legs. Endless threads of perspiration hang like honey from the coating of my flesh. Grabbing my atlas, turning the page, charting the faster path to somewhere.

Breath pressing hard from my belly, now is unadorned by anything except the hard pulsating of my own heart. Melting crevices of my flesh, as heat rises like a raging fire careening down my legs. Relationship begins to evolve between self and sneakers...

Finding my breath through flesh and heat, sipping sweat like a cocktail. Beads of perspiration begin to fashion on my upper arm. Feeling cement beneath my feet, pulse resting in the center of my chest. Slick with sweat, humming along. Using my arms as shovels to scoop through the air. My toe, mostly bare, as a damp blanket of body dew covers it's intrusion, into cool crisp early morning air. I've stepped out of myself, in a relationship with the hole in my sneaker...

Running hard, sweating wildly. My skin burning underneath like a soft pear cooked to a boil.

A bird fly's up, breathing the sugar smell of my skin, thirsty for my salt. Honey vapor fills the sky, pixilation of goddess hands reach down and wipe my brow. My bones, held together by flesh and heat, my breath, the drug itself, seems harmless, as feet dance along, slicing through the air. The pulse radiates from the center of my chest, as beads of my own body, run the course along the inner side of my arm. The ridge of euphoria now touches the edge of my fingertips. Relationship of feet and sneakers...

My sneakers, unlike me, lack the audacity to mythologize their life. They are simply insipidly entranced, not nearly human enough to comprehend the passage of time, or fear, or the onslaught of the fragility of it all. They are leather and cloth, as each morning I hold them, in a tight embrace of the laces. Their life, held firmly in the perfuse smell of a wretched sweat. I push them harder, then they need to be pushed, them, being compliant in the exertion. Each one, one more step closer between heaven and hell, as leather reshapes on each step of a stone.

Myself, finding a benefit to pushing beyond myself, my laces, not so much. Dancing carelessly to the music of the wind, sipping morning tea in droplets from my pores. Impinging on my toe, a small hole, as toe plays a game of peek-a-boo amid the morning's air. Looking downward, undaunted by the exposure to air, my toe makes an immediate non-negotiable exit from the blanket of my sneaker. As my steps pound the earth, my toe becomes the great observer.

Freedom of being unclothed, as my toe stands in unknown abyss, as toe, now revels in the moment. No more refusing the invitation to hurl itself into full exposure, or into the depths of my innermost world, poignantly mentioning, it is well tired of being held to the fire in a morning ritual of overheated flesh. No longer thundering, the tear in the canvas grows ever wider, as I run in softened step. My toe, now breathing in my breath, in a freedom from it's caging...

The natural temperament of my sneakers today is a slow methodical pace. Just enough cool crisp air, as a deer studies the bone structure of my face. Terracing down towards the river, sun organically falling from the ceiling, I bath in the rays. Birds with elephant ears grab hold of my whispers, as chosen secrets spill in silent confession.

Seductive soft restraint of my flesh, embraced by each pearl of sweat, seductively caresses the curves of my body. Stolen glimpse of forbidden thought. Listening to birds, licking off dewdrops, suckling, once again, I begin to grow. Bridging the gap, stepping over stones, piecing together my path. An almost palpable energy, gliding in, as

sky lies flat in an unimaginable blue.
Sun dips upon the salt encrusted on my
body, warm blood flowing like wine.
    Mouth wide open, pink tongue
lolling on drips of my body's perfume.
Legs unwind down the hill, as laces
unfurl on intoxication of the breeze...

    The offensiveness of the wind, as the
storm rolls over my sneakers, laces left
abandoned at the door. The outside air
becoming a lost city of sorts, broken
into pieces, then glued back together.
Limbs, trees, bones, scattered, I find
my thoughts cohere around the waterfall
spilling from the sky. Sneakers sit,
ornamental, there is no way out, only
in. Out the door, my arms reaching,
catching air with barren hands, as fingers
wash in the sky's river. Touching the bones
in my face, fingertips leaving drops on my
cheeks. Rain falling like a bucket dumped,
as my sneakers ache for a sunny sky.
Listening to the drops, I edge into

breath, something heavy falling off of me, as my heart becomes a low level vibration. Rain continuously pelts, unannounced, its lashing is left unceasing of time and place.

My sneakers stand, peering through the glass, waiting, amid the drowning...

Sweat, a sort of medicinal cleansing, a red antiseptic poured over wounds. The morning light is shady. Humidity and desire an inside – out tangle on my flesh. I swallow dry, as my pores drip. I know to keep moving, if I stop, I'll wake from the euphoria. Gold floats from the wood of the trees, the day's opening, the opposite of every place I have ever been.

Clouds envelope me like an array of endless white scarves, extending down in rawness, a calm before the storm. Giving my breathing time to regulate, legs burning less, face, now flush and red. Scrutinizing dew drops as they spill on

the pavement, watching the fill and
pour, over and over.

Breath opens wider, almost pulling
in the teary sullenness of the cloud
swept sky. Running faster, in a quickening
of pace, riding out the calm before the
storm... as I close the door, in secluded
embrace with my sneakers.

Someone is now speaking to me
directly, asking a question from the
other side of somewhere, as I pick up
my pencil drawing answer across the sky.
Clouds roll in from above, my indicator
of silence, in the coolest of morning
air. I'm thirsty for the taste of my own
salt, feeling amorphous, like a cloud
or the ocean. Falling backward into a
jubilant echolocation, the deer, clamoring
to be noticed by me. The ridge of my
body standing on the edge, so calm in a
currency of breath, as body dew is the
coat I wear. Something seismic shifts
inside of me, as the rooms of my body

shift into a new place. Feeling the ground under my feet, running into my life, my bones lifting, separate, under the humid sheen of my flesh. The air, the way it announces itself, smoldering, pavement slants, sneakers slip, as I come to rest on the stonewall.

The heat increasing, rising to a baking temperature, I'm drenched, emptying my water bottle on my tongue, as the mirage slips from my fingertips...

The drone of air dissolves in the gentle splashing of water that cascades down my flesh. My sophisticated drip-by-drip irrigation system, efficiently delivers water to all my roots, as leftover spills from my pores. My feet meander the path, as sullen dark cloud bursts form in the distance. Symmetry reigns supreme, as each cloud lends a sense of order to the boisterous black lining of the sky. Sneakers creep ahead of the storm, pausing to stand in the stillness of the sullen air.

My legs, my mirrored soul, as I pull
back and up the hill. Falling on my skin,
droplets rush in, as the force of the
breeze tugs at me, insistent I am not
alone today. The escalation of nature,
in a changing shift, a breeze removing
fragments once in my path. A sparrow
takes hold beside me, flying on a sea
of self-evocation, riding a wave into
the rain, as fog shrouds the treetops.
Paintbrush dribbling colors on the
sidewalk, my breath now a scarlet red.

The abyss into which nighttime
has fallen now fades, as the daylight
brings the cleansing. A little reckless,
almost righteous, honey beams cascade
in a direct hit against my shoulders.
The sea, reflected in the sky, as the
slightest of breeze blows upon me.
Playing hide and seek with my thoughts,
pulling the sunshine down, illusions
begin to stray. Exuded in the ambiance

of a new day unfolding, as the world still shelters in the darkness of the night. Heightening the slicing of my breath through the air, as sneakers cough and sputter in a concentrated downhill escalation. Sneakers succumb to time and place breath softens the strong angles of existence.

The goal to return transformed, each new end, proves to be my gift of engagement with every crossroad reality. The sun is now twinkling through the slightest of branches. The solitude of the dirt remains profoundly empowering. Serendipitous diffusion, as my senses allow me to make sense out of the cool air which now floats along my flesh. Quintessential art of the pulsating of my veins, in tune with the rhythm of my feet, allows an echo to resound from my soul.

My feet land on the unsteadiness of the pebbles, transitioning my legs back

to a place of grace. Morning dew capsules
fall from the tree onto my shoulders.
Nakedly exposing every nuance about me
in the run, as weathered chains drop to
the pavement. Releasing my breath, as
a fire quickly ignites from my navel
traveling south down the burn of my
legs. Ligaments glisten in beads of pearls,
as salt coats the canvas of my body.

The smell of my body waifs upon
my nostrils, as the burn rolls down
my brow. A bluebird swoops down,
in a feathered touch, whisking away
the droplets on my cheek. Seduced by
the notion, that they hold my secrets,
he drinks the moisture from my lips,
like a fine wine. Wings reaching, sweetly
I surrender, fragile, innocent, safe,
for an instant... a self-portrait of my
lost and found.

In depth conversation, gentle
detoxify, on the cusp of a saturated
breath. A chiming of bells spills from

my windpipe, as life no longer beige,
but a tapestry of color, today, a Chilean
red. Salt coats the crushed red pepper
of my heated flesh. The over heated
symphony runs as a river, dancing my
fears on the exposure of air. Seduced
by the sumptuousness, sipping sweat,
as if it were a fine aged wine, there for
the quenching. Tasting on the idea of
letting go...

I think the birds in flight call my
name, as their simple melody begins to
paint across the sky. Sun bright, breeze
flat, my body remaining in perfect
symmetry with breath. Remarking at the
timelessness of the hill, as sweat
bathes over my flesh. Anchored in the
view of my conservatory, droplets hang
from feathers of the trees, each bead
of breath sitting on a throne of air.
Indulgent in the stillness of scarlet
breath. A pair of birds in full animation,
escort me to the river's edge. I am

inside and out, and outside and in, all in the same breath. Air bites crisp on the soothing repetition of steps. I am floating on a wing and a prayer, as sweat forms on the indulgence; sneakers behave in another time and place.

Cool morning air, falls upon my shoulders, catching the "bittersweet" of life's surrenders. Times of holding conjoin with times of letting go. Sun streaks through last night's sullen skies. In a heated embrace, my sneakers launch onto an isolated path, enclosed in a morning mist that falls like rain upon my exposed flesh.

Footing leaving imprints, a map of where I have been, and how to find me. Nostrils flare on each inhalation, as the heaving of my chest reaches up to the sun. Breath keeping pace with the pulsing of my heart, fears are left curbside. Reaching hand backward, flecking a bead of sweat from dribbling down a

shoulder blade. The corner of my eye
catches a perfect white rose extending
its tongue, on the coolest of air. Thorns
now stand at attention, assuming the
piercing on the slightest of touch. A
pulsating dribble of red adds intrusion
to the salted waters running from my
pores, a droplet lies upon my sneaker.

I think I hear the air move, steadily
fluttering across my back, a calm
pushing my body forward. Listening only
to the beating of my own heart, as I
close my eyes to the rest of the world,
rejecting even a momentary thought. The
heat in my legs having a voice of it's
own, as I step rhythmically through
the pattern. Columns of sweat run the
river of my body, as my navel pools the
tide, and the coarseness of salt pinches
at my flesh. Sneakers move, as the
penchant of standing still is no longer
a welcoming option.
    The silence of the morning air is now

broken, as breath evokes on a bird's song. A profusion of English Garden tea roses overlaps my path, a threshold to some new beginning... as breath forms a cluster of diamonds, stepping from skin, leaving the world behind, in an unsung song that awaits for me tomorrow...

As soon as I move, I hear the sound of the waves, the sea now appeasing my soul. Curving pathways echo off of large standing stones. Vowing to just stand in this place and 'be', a moment of solace, as dawn breaks on the closing of the moon. Yesterday is cast away... today's breath is just beginning, as I anchor myself firmly in my sneakers for the audacious uphill climb, as my salted waters spill out onto the pavement. Lost, or simply nearing to be found!

Forever reminded in the silence of the trees, of life's turbulent waves and gusty winds; always cautious, as the water can be bitingly cold and the currents notoriously strong. The sun, the color of fine red wine, a touch of decadent color flourishes amid the hypnotic effect of passing clouds caught in the corner of my eye. Everywhere my breath finds me, walls are adorned with my serene canvasses, as thoughts explode against a ribbon of sky. A thousand miles have past amid a freezing wind and here I am, here I remain, among copper walls and an antiquated china blue scroll of sky. Do I dare attempt to run tip toed over the horizon, or in a thunderous clapping of my feet, so all can be heard?

Quietly stepping into my artist eyes, as glamorous hues of pink turn to gold upon the sun rising. Framing poetic verse across the sky, not so much a desire for me as it is a necessity. A deep yearning to appease my soul, as I try to listen with eyes closed, to hear the sound of a distant sea, somewhere. The shape made by the trees makes me feel as if I am running into an embrace. The run now comes together holistically, not particularly planning the route. I, pretending to be neither a mermaid of Zen nor, the sky. A backdrop of sea, wheeling birds flying through the waves, adding to the drama of production unfolding. My breath equates with drops of mist from the trees, as my tongue extends on the indulgence. Calm, cool, simplicity of pace keeps me from falling off the cliffs...

Stripped down to flesh, coated in rain, serenity now. Sprawled on breath, eyes closed, I concentrate on the surrounding sounds: trickling rain, rhythmic whisper of breath, strains of sweat carried on the breeze. Braced for the interruption of the puddles, as my feet enjoy the reverie. Hearing the distant giggle of a deer, downshifting into a carefree languor rarely reached this short into a run. I am gleefully childlike in this oasis. The crushed – glass fire pit of sun peacefully nodding off, slothful against the sullen sky of rain. A soundtrack of chirping heard in the distance, as I can feel on my face the border between the water and the air. Hearing an ocean, somewhere, still washing ashore, and the calmer beating of my own heart.

My sneakers as boats, as I navigate the flooded streets. Rain pelting, piercing shoulder blades, like electrical currents traveling the whole of my body. My breath caught up in the shock waves, as my body submits to the punishing. Torrents of rain filling my sneakers, watching water crashing, as the mapping of the pavement becomes my idyllic middle ground.

The paradox is running, and yet standing still, amid the rain. Release and cleansing, in a peppery red spice of air, now resting on my tongue on each exhalation. Hitting the wall, as my body angles down, ushering me into an enveloped interior of self. I knock on the gate, still a bit unsure, the air ushers me in, as I fall silent on the whisper of a raindrop. My secret recipe of self - indulgence.

Leaving behind the twinkling stars of night, as moon shifts to daylight. Standing in this place, no words needed to speak, quiet is all I need. Strong hands of the flowers standing up, sometimes, when I can, no longer.

I swore I would ask the birds, but words just don't come easily. How do I part the clouds, to find the silver lining? A poet in paint, as I float. My silhouette sharply illuminated by an early sun, against a purplish sky.

Trees still plunged in darkness, in shifting, almost willful moodiness. The sundry bark of the trees and flower petals still seem partially asleep. Finding peace in the run, creating a formal harmony, a sort of diamond that flatters and then ravishes my soul. I am suspended in impeccably controlled poetic breath...

In the science of survival it is the acceptance of the reality of my life, and the will to live each day to the fullest, that I purge from my sneakers. A life span measured in weeks, months and years, with the ability to reach acceptance influenced by the quality, meaning, and value that I place on my life.

The only certainty in life is that it will end for all of us, eventually. It is a painful thought, but acknowledging it helps me focus on what is really important, what I want to accomplish.

The air so calm this morning, it's a song poured down my throat. Chimes left in the wind, jangle at every corner. Sneakers echoing and sputtering up the hill. Blowing each breath back, as if I am filling balloons. Navigating the bored stares of the deer, already settled in their grazing. My throat now level with their eyes, as the song pours down. My body heated, as the sun asks me punishing questions I am not prepared for. Running only as far as the sky is blue...

The sun's rays like a tip of a razor against my skin. Spanish moss now hangs as hair in the morning air. The air is so familiar, angular, a bit less humid. It is as if my sneakers are now carrying me. The force field is lifting just long enough for me to hear the voice of the bluebird. Rolling off a cliff, jaded and shaded, a question for the bluebird sitting on the window ledge, do we change life, or does life change us? Touching my breath to the keyhole of a door I don't know how to open, as sneakers touch down on the grass. Paying attention to the unseen, as my body empties it's water bottle onto my tongue. Scattered photographs strewn across the sky...

Spine surging forth from the anchor of my legs, pulling so far back into my body that I do not know who I am, my breath, the thread now weaving mind and soul. My dam is open as the water from my pores runs the length of my river bed, flesh now pelted by my river's rains. Allowing self to sway, to pause, dropping breath from forehead to groin. Looking up into the blue ribbon of sky, getting lost, allowing self to be empty, only then can my voice emerge.

Falling, retrieving, balancing...
unsung songs
now touch my sound
forever lost
forever found...

High a top a tree, a solemn bird in a lace collared red shirt bears a poetic offering. Glinting with barely – there sun beams extending through. The catalyst, something deeper is driving my breath in the heating of the morning air. The bird in red coat now rests on my shoulder, a release of water from my pores, not certain of the tear releasing from the bird. A wing, wipes away my indignities, revealing grace on my brow, the curious paradox of accepting self as I am, then I change.

Twined in life, leaving imprints on all I touch, small drizzles of color surround me, aesthetically driven, poetically literate, serene, eccentric and wonderful. Happily grounded in my sneakers...

Having a quite obvious affinity for the things I like, and fearlessness in my composition of style. Compositions restrained and harmonious evolving and adapting to the passage of time and the change in my life. My sense of serenity is heightened in the unfolding view. Worry is sometimes subtle and insidious. Life, out of my hands, not a single thing more can I do, moving through life from one worry to the next is wasted energy. Breath dances naked across the fabric of sky...

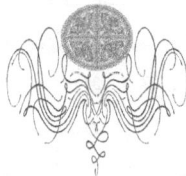

What was once bold here is now subtle, what was energetic now calm, seemingly completely new, pushed in different directions, amid muted shades of pewter, silver and gray, sky is transformed, exotic thoughts strewn upon a gray linen wall. An indigo blue sky stands perfectly against breath, as more intimately scaled thoughts arrive in a familiar location. Happily replete in the view of the deer, as a pool of sweat splashes at my feet, pores now opening up their flood gates in the release.

Poetry of summer in champagnes and raspberry pinks, channel my layers of movement. Do I run, or do I float? Moments are clouds in a photograph. The turning of a page, facing away from the sea, breath now fully inhaled. My arms extend as wings, as my voyage hungers to happen. A prayer for silence and fertile rain, as stillness becomes my sneakers instrument. Year by year is still not clear yet day by day, I find my way at the interface of runner and wanderer.

Clustering diamonds of breath precede me. Thanking my feet for the miles they have tread, and the profusion of sweat frozen in time. Closing eyes to see, sun on my back, as legs draw closer to conclusion, clearing cobwebs along my path.

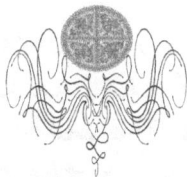

Thoughts of the sea release a needed calm, against the backdrop of a vibrant red heat. Words set to emotion, as emotion validates through my sneakers. Wrestling with complexities, brick walls I am climbing. Just beneath my surface, barely spoken curves of breath fan my cheek, loosing my grip in the moment. A nameless ravine whispers over me. Antique worn surfaces of self, blend thoughts as they spill out onto the harsh of the pavement. My glass walls turn to turquoise sea glass, languishing on thoughts to private to explore. Each piece of glass, a broken piece I plant as a seedling, as I drift on a current of newfound air. Circumnavigating the contradictions, making sense of disparate pieces, as heat settles in every pore. My sneakers now drenched by the soaking...

The absence of rain this morning has left the heat of the sun warming the flesh of my face. The beads of my salty sweat, mixed in with the cascades of the waterfalls streaming from my eyes. The warmth changing the identity of what once was, a cold rain, into a new season of life, my life. Setting fire to a new sense of spirit, in which the process of rising up can only begin from within. Mitigating around the glass pieces, carefully watching each unturned stone... somewhere between the end and the point that I began, is my journey. A journey unfolding before me... a path not crystal clear as I pause to dislodge a piece of embedded jaded glass from my sneaker. I see the drop of blood... the glass has silently let me know, it was there...

The rain is my endless cloth of creativity. Washing down on me, washing through me, all things composed, written across miles of a beaten path. Flesh so wet, under a blanket of rain, birds look at me in condemnation. My toes now pinging on every squish of my sneaker...

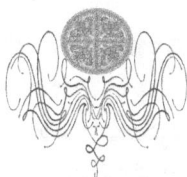

A river of puddles washes over my sneaker; as my own river of wetness, adds to the drowning. A fallen leaf floats away on single breath columns of humidity that trace the air. Outpouring from the Gods, tears from distant lost angels, now dampen my silhouette. Lost in the entrancement.

Poetry of my body in fluid motion, as my writing takes on verse across the sky. In contempt, a deer stands in my crossing. Eyes gazed, breath fixed. Humidity rests as a blanket, on my shoulders, as my waterspouts open their gates for the drowning. The drenching has begun.

My head prorates forward, as if my brain needs to arrive before my legs. Daunting color spectrum of the horizon, something deeper drives the shifting of the air. Am I floating, or caught in an embrace?

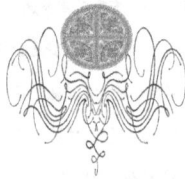

The earlier I begin the day, the quieter the sound. Reverberations of my own renderings, caught in the patter, as sneakers hit the pavement. Trees lay still, sky asleep, mornings dew resting on an eyelash. Pulsating of my heart, my only sound; liquid pours down my back in beads of isolated seclusion...

Epilogue

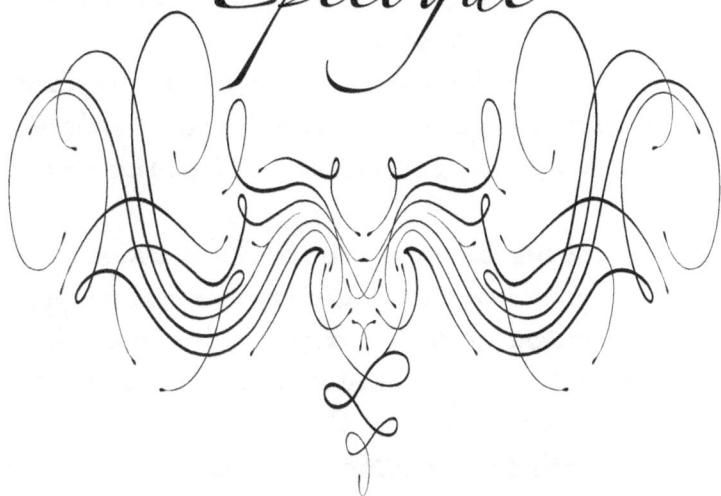

Through all the miles,
all the early morning runs,
my sneakers have become
the breathtaking force
shaping my life. Birds hear
my confession daily, taking hold of the
steel and feathers that make me. My
arms extend out as wings for whatever
ails me. No matter how it is my
beginning, always ending in a graceful
flight. I could be a permanent gypsy
without much thought, never staying
long enough to tire. Each day I am
always turning, yet, another page of life.
Spending much time upside down, and

inside out, my sneakers anchor me amid all of the intrusions.

I use to be a pickled cypress infused with bits of gold, a chalky thirsty look, now I am a sunlit gallery of beautiful art.

As some people are lucky enough to have a corridor in which to run through, my experiences have become, for me, my ornate stepping-stones leading me daily to who knows where.

The poetry of life, as I know all too well, often births from the most unlikely places. Through all the darkness came the rendering of color. The rebuilt relationship with my sneakers, as I learned, once again, how to run, as part of my rehabilitation. Finding peace in the solitude of the clicking off of strokes of my keyboard, and the wet dampness of my sneakers, poetically literate, serene, eccentric and wonderful, giving birth to the writing that now paints my life!

Giving thanks to my sneakers each time they take flight.

Go for a run at the crack of dawn, exist solely within yourself, smell the air, feel the breeze, hear the silence, allow the beating of your own heart to be the rhythm of your feet.

It is only then, that you will truly have learned, what it is to be tamed by your own breath. It is in that moment of the emptiness of thought, that I became a better version of self. It is in the silence... that I broke thunderous ground.

I encourage all of you to do the same.

Lillian Jade

Continue reading for a
preview of the upcoming novel
by Lillian Jade

Naked

in front of God

Book 1

Coming in Spring 2012

MY EYES FLICKER OPEN TO THE SUN NOW shining in the bedroom window, as a small puddle begins to pool on my window to the world. I enter into conversation with my husband with bravado, as mood swings could erupt shouting, that would stream across large continents. As I brave the topic of leaving work, my image of self is about to be completely altered. The now ugly force excreting from my head is suddenly neutralizing confidence in my future abilities. Changing so rapidly, no longer even recognizable to me, is the person in the mirror. Signs were everywhere.

Positive that my head would eventually explode, pain and pressure greater than anything I had ever experienced in all my years. In the midst of all the chaos, no one noticed the shrinking of me. Denial is a great contender.

... My world begins to slant

Saddest departure from once I went

Sadness Moves In As My New Tenant

MY SOLITUDE ALLOWS ME TO WEEP, AS I often do, and to drain the anger and sadness from my blood. My grief, sewn into my skin, weaved into a fabric of how much I have already lost. Searching for hope in darkened dreams, my throat so choked up there is no longer passage of air. Nighttime restlessness is a masquerading despair, as my world becomes my tomb. Dark circles under my eyes, as I am ready to drop to the floor, the depression coupled with lack of sleep, colliding into a foreseen train wreck up ahead. My skin cold, my heart lifeless, I think about an eternal sleep. My body rearranges itself; smell surrounds me in suffocating paltriness of dried crusted blood, adding to the pillage of the zigzag stitches yanking at my brain. All consuming is the smell of the blood. The pattern on my scalp, darkened circles of my eyes, the tomb I am slowly falling prey to, washing my face with the splash of cold water at the bathroom sink, tauntingly glancing in the mirror. Dark threads run trails across my flesh, crusts of day old blood flake upon touch. The urge to pick the crusts intensifies, as if to remove them will change the view in the mirror.

I nap during the day; I miss breathing, my own scent, my soft eyes, and my need for him. I miss the sprawl of his body as we now sleep alone, as the leakage from the sutures drains on the bed sheets. Lace camisoles, night time indulgences, soft lips on my skin, fingers running along the inside of my thighs, god how I miss all of those sweet things. The incessant smell of the blood demandingly fills my senses, rising into my nostrils, as I bury my face in the pillow to escape the intoxicating fumes. Running my hand over the ridge of my neck, searching for a pulse, verifying I am still alive.

My prescriptions begin to resemble the starting line up of a baseball team, (Neurontin, Tylenol with codeine, Zoloft, Percocet, Gabapentin, Vicodin,

Clorazepam, Klonopin, Lyrica, Lorazepam, Cym-
balta, steroid injections: I think at some point, someone even threw in a Valium for good measure; my
arsenal of assault weapons in added dosage)

Listing the dosage and time for each one, dutifully writing out a schedule. Laboring in determination I get down the flight of stairs, positioning my
lean against the banister, searching for the glass
of water I left somewhere. Cold droplets of ice water travel the journey of my tongue, giving passage
to my feast of morning pills. Eggs a daughter had
made me before heading off to school, now sit cold
and hard as nausea rises from my belly. My olfac-
tory sense ignites the part of my brain that puts
me right back into the smell of the hospital, as
blood vessels swell in my eyes and I try not to cry.
It is the eggs and the dried day old blood fusing together in a putrid revisit to the metal and steel of
the operating room. Scents change to fear and sadness where rage and frustration have settled in. Ex-
hausted from what seems like a journey into the
land of the dead. Hearing the sweetest sounds of
the ocean near my window, I close my eyes, daring
to remember when the world had been mine, cup-
ping my palm against my cheek; pills are dissolv-
ing me into a much-needed sleep.

I think my dog smells my sadness in a way that
others can't. Welcoming the thought of her sooth-

ing tongue, wondering is she would attempt to lick my wounds while I slept, as dogs often are drawn to a source of blood.

Four days have past, my head pressed deeply in my pillow, sutures matted to flesh, imprinting my pillow with blood. My skin cells shed spreading out over my pillowcase. Feeling the crush of coldness chilling my spine, as I reach down for the white thermal hospital blanket my body had been carried home in. Expecting at least God to understand my grief, not wanting to open up to family around me. Private conversations, in isolated corners of my brain, I beg for his mercy in failed attempts at subduing the pain. I need empathy, at least from God!

Just lying here and breathing, has become such a daily accomplishment, I can't even remember what really matters anymore. My work has had to come to an end. It gave me structure to stroll into the office each day, task at hand, always mitigating some project or legal proposal. I had stayed on track for a bit more than a year now since the accident, although with the help of sedatives, and a small heater provided me to counteraction the onset of the central air on my scalp. Bandanas have become my accessory item of choice, protection and a need to hide the grotesque in public spaces. I am positive to the complete stranger; I am in chemotherapy treatment hiding my head from the shame.

They would never understand the nature of the freakishness of what has happened to me. The continual purposeless taunting needs to be deleted from my brain.

Someone now pestering me as to how long to treat my panic attacks, as I harbor as a prisoner in my home for the duration. They tell me two more years. I tell them, just let me die. Let me close my eyes in eternal sleep. I know death stops pain.

Summers heat matting my scalp with dried blood, sutures, and day old perspiration. I am becoming raged in my own disgust. My bathing needs to be supervised, as I loose balance under the water. Wanting to stand under Niagara Falls, anointing my forehead as the water cascades down my head over my breasts, round the curvature of my belly, down my thighs, pooling the blood in a release at my feet. After the cleansing, closing my eyes, breathing into him, tasting his mint toothpaste, my brain falsifying my delusions.

I still feel the rasp of the breathing tube in my mouth from the operation, the force of anesthesia seeping through my veins, ever mindful of green cotton scrubs standing over me. Aware of how all of my senses keep reverting back to the coldness of the steel, the ungodly smell of blood and recovery. Pressing my lips together, attempting to stop their vibration and the tears that are running through my body. Wishing the doctor had simply cut off my head and sewn it up, so as not to be able to think, taste, smell or breathe. Shaking uncontrollably, I slide further under my blanket. Is someone home with me? Anyone? Pain the only message being offered to my body from my brain. The audacity to assume this can simply employ mind over matter. What the hell? Audible howls of near death intoxicating pain, begging from the deepest pockets of my soul.

Awkwardly getting one leg up and on the floor, working up the energy to carry my remains to the bathroom. Emptying my bladder enough to finally sleep, neither sad nor afraid, I am simply empty. Lying back in my recovery place, curled in a fetal position, aloneness runs through me in torrent cycles.

Deep moans jerk my body as I attempt to sprawl to the kitchen. I am quite sure my daughter's note read that she had made me a sandwich, and had left it on the refrigerator shelf. I am sitting on the kitchen floor as the dizziness has landed me in a momentary land of madness. The god-awful selection of pills selectively sitting next to my sandwich, the continued antidote for anxiety and pain. The balloons inserted into my scalp need to remain calm, the pills allowing me to step off the shores of reality. Tightly clenching the sandwich, as an equivalent of grief passes through my ribcage.

The absurdity of my life now seems so hollow, as if I have somehow shrunk in size. Straining to open the window, so the breeze can pick me up and land me someplace else. The smell of the sea salt as it revives my deadened senses. I never thought that hopelessness could be felt, it not only can, it aches inside like a raging storm. Falling back onto the couch, as mounting the stairs to the bedroom seems to be audacious, I lie in sweat.

My oldest daughter will be home soon from her job, presumably to stare blankly at me, not knowing what to say. It has become her defensive to keep herself unshaved from my reality. I understand her need. I understand the need to stand bathed in sunlight in the sound of your own heartbeat. The complete suppressing of thought and fears.

Brushing an escaping tear from the corner of my eye, I don't think the drugs are working today. Sadness has taken up residence on a bolstered sofa inside my ribs, holding a cocktail in hand, and not leaving anytime soon. Prying secrets from me today, will take an ungodly act of will. I'm shutting down, and in desperate need of some water, my legs do not want to move from the couch. When will the lightheadedness end? Or when it ends, will I end too?

Tears are waterfalls of cleansing...

ITTING IN THE WAITING ROOM, ALREADY FEEL-
ing the pinching and pulling as stitches
are to be removed today. With eyes
squeezed shut and nostrils flared, I yogic
breathe through the removal. Done. "You wait a
week or so, and then we will again begin the process
of the filling. Once healing of the implant is success-
ful." I take the doctors words wishing the whole human race would just go to hell. My son now driving me home, couch pillows fluffed around my head,
as the car vibrations are something my head can
no longer endure. Stopping at the pharmacy, which
in effect has become my small time neighborhood
drug lord. Cohesively sabotaging my world pharmaceuticals abound. Yellow ones for this; white ones
for that, and a spectacle of capsules for everything
else. Mumbling that he needs to get to work, my son
delivers me home. Arranging all my inherent would
be needs around me, within my arms reach, he now
closes the door behind him.

My bedroom has the best view out to the sea, facing Lighthouse Island watching boats and storms
creep across the sky. Sudden despair sets in, no other
soul in the house, the dog's footsteps my only expec-
tation. These are the worst moments of my day, an
endurance of dry throat choking back my tears. The

port on the back of my head squeezing tightly toward the front of my eye, kidnapping thoughts too bizarre to repeat to another living soul.

How grotesque I look, my body smell altered, no longer mine. Everything I eat tastes metallic, swear it is the pharmaceuticals encroaching on my taste buds. I have failed to save myself, from the onset of fear and the disruption of life. I fall asleep on the couch purring faint noises from my breath, pigeon toed seconds of pain in a sleep-induced state.

The first two weeks have past; I am paused in relief, each day leading closer to closure. In a love hate relationship with my surgeon. I judge his strength by the small points of pain where his finger has pressed against my flesh. Saline solution delivered through the port, 12 ccs as the local anesthetic numbs the skin but the internal pressure mounts. Yogic breathing gets me through the duration. I no longer know who I am, the face in the mirror with a protrusion high above my scalp. Nauseated, I cannot even regard a sprinkling of conversation on the car ride back home. My scalp so tight I think a bursting flood is only moments away.

My dog lies next to me near the couch, commiserating with my discomfort. Dependent on the very people whom are suppose to be dependent on me, my children. Dutifully each daughter bounds in making awkward small talk, the surprise in their eyes on the now protrusion from my head. My scalp appearing as if it is in the first stages of gestation, as hatching is still a few weeks away. An alien might appear, green and slimy with octopus arms and legs. Or it might be a pure white dove.

Always darkest in the mid of night

Family Abruptions

EXTENDED FAMILY INTERACTIONS NEVER WERE anything more than a horde of scandals, petty jealousies, and a lifelong solitary confinement of family secrets. One by one, family arrives, breaching national security I am sure. Taking care of my brother, signing the lease, as I promised I would do, outrage melts down my neck muscles as I am asked to do the impossible, once again. I have helped to rent him a little cottage down the street from me, on a narrow strip between the beaches. Bad choices seem to have landed him in predicament again. I am his "Good Ship" bail out. Dutifully, I affix my pen to co sign the legal document.

Everybody leaves not wanting to hear about the saddest parts of my now daily life. Most of my family, at odds with each other, narcissism runs deep in our line of lineage. Someone always baiting a trap for someone, this time around, I am sure, is to be no different.

The morning smelling of seashells and dried seaweed, as I no longer recognize the face in the mirror. My face is bloated from medications, my eyes sullen from lack of sleep, and the weight of the balloon on the top of my head awkwardly clumsy for comfort. Skin graft stretched so tight I could easily be popped, thus releasing a surge of helium into the air. Then I could suck up the air and change my voice, and somehow pretend to be someone else. The ugliness of the contraption now frightens me.

Opening up the bathroom window, blowing out the ghosts who think they can take over my body. Picking from an array of bandanas and scarves, shielding my scalp from the rays touching down on my deck, opportunistically eyeing the view of the sea. Once again, today is camera day. Another vogue moment of head protrusions to be shot, my breasts somehow ending up as pointed soldiers in the pictures. My tiny breasts so left behind, altered, lonely for attention, caressing in the night ended with the first deluge of blood and sutures. Sleeping in curled fetal position, positioning my protrusions elevated on three pillows, convulsiveness of sexual interaction no longer a reasonable option.

I miss being touched, as much as I miss doing

the feeling. Following the sound of the sea, sitting on my deck, tumbling over the edge of a now shadowy existence. The sun slowing me into a trance, as my mid day feast of prescriptions easily slides down my throat. No one ever exactly reads the warnings on the side of pill bottles, as the shear frightening hell of the side effects would surely never allow us to consciously fill the illegible scribble in the first place.

One of my hands writes in black ink across the blank page of my journal, putting information together as carefully as I can. Compiling what I know of my life so far. Charting events in a timeline since the accident. Doodling fills some of the pages, drawings of three-dimensional tiny squares, prisms, some lines connecting the intricate patterns, in between, verses of poetry. I feel oversized in conversation, often just playfully doodling with pencil and paper, a way of avoidance, I suppose. Less confidant, threshed in the isolation of the house, making meager of my social skills.

Feeling something sharp and painful between my shoulder blades, as the fear begins to creep downward into my spine. Something right in the here and now, drops from my throat to my stomach, I am afraid of the pain. I am all knowing of the hollow needle that will suck at my flesh. The knife I imagine cold cutting my threaded skin. Another audacious surgery is waiting in the wings. My heart now beating so fast, it becomes motorized. Fears once again, begin to mount. Lifting a glass of water, so cold, the ice cuts against my lips. A wave folds back over me holding hand open to the ocean, I am a ravenous seabird. No one yet aiming the scalpel knife at me, again; but a diagrammed entrance into my flesh awaits me, tomorrow. A flashing light will go off, and my body will be delivered underground, breaking me in a way that will push me further inside myself, a consequence of the volcanic ash pumped through my veins.

What dragon will I have to slay tomorrow?

Dragons in absent of fairytales

Gurney Awaits Me

*I*T IS TIME AGAIN; I KISS MY HUSBAND GOODBYE as the gurney rolls me down the corridor. Their hands slide around me as I am lifted onto the operating table. Round two, to disassemble the implant, graft down a centimeter of skin, reposition a new expander, thus beginning again, the refilling and stretching with saline solution over the next few weeks. Sensing I may somehow stop breathing as the oxygen mask is positioned over my face, alcohol swabs on my arm, conditioning the sterility of the vein, the anesthesia drip begins to float my world. The kaleidoscope is spinning furiously in my brain, as the colors break off into pictures of my life, as I am headed down that metal staircase, somewhere between heaven and hell. It must be hell, as I cannot escape the vivid smell of the room.

Pushing open the door to the recovery room where postoperative I lie, a nurse swabs my forehead. I am chilled, but in a complete breakout of sweat. My body is adhering to the trauma and shock, readjusting as I emerge again in the real world. The gauze wrapped in mummy attire around my head, wincing from the slightest indication of a hand on mine. Feeling his breath near my nose, as a feathered kiss lands on my lips, awakening like sleeping beauty. My husband standing over me, fogged from the anesthetic, the bright lights hurt my eyes. Gritting my teeth I cannot speak, as he wipes a tear rolling down my cheek. The powerful, mind altering drugs, begin to empty from my body. I don't have the strength to sit up yet, as I heave in a bedpan. Each heave penetrating the deepest part of my core, as my head sways in circles of confusion. His world has been pulled apart; the lightning strike of my accident has taken away all that he loved. The stare of his eyes, in a predestined heart attack mode, as his loss is uncontainable. Standing over me, as if to say,

"I belong to someone, I miss someone, and you need to come back to me." I no longer had the power to fill his request. The surgery was messy, complicated. It had removed even more of my necrotic flesh.

Sliding me into the car, wrapping his arms around my rib cage, lifting and placing me in the front seat. Feeling the need to now urinate, a towel is placed under my rear end, just in case. Reaching over gingerly placing his hand on my thigh futile attempts at soothing the pain. The hapless map of the road leading us home, every bump we hit, is met with a tear. I am a form of tangled vines as my dog, in a sniffing pant, meets us at the house, she recognizes the blood, and moans in tune with me. She sleeps next to me, by the front door, as if protective of intruders.

Deflation of Lungs and Withering of Heart

*T*HE SLUR THAT HAS OVERTAKING MY speech, has made me inebriate to the world. The puffiness to my face, largely a consequence of prescribed medications for the duration of my surgeries. All of us are afraid of acknowledging the substance of truth, so, simply, we don't. Not letting life be a sad tale of justification and wasted potential, the realization that none of us walk on water, is probably one of the most feared fears we each hold. The outside world having their own less than fairytale version and interpretation of us all. Extended family crap now ferments with acidic vapors, just barley falling short of suicidal mania.

The man in the cottage serenely sitting down on the edge of the bed, waiting to be saved by God, trusting me with his life. I smile at him, as he blows out any remaining air from his lungs, on his last cigarette. I slip my hand under his hind quarters in a masterful attempt to direct him to the bathroom. Not wanting him to get myself, or him, wet in the crossing. With a curdled howl he sits on the toilet, as if every bone in his body is breaking on the onset, falling slightly sideways.

Wrapped in thermal blankets and strapped to a stretcher they escort his body out to the ambulance. In a fever pitch to inflate his lungs, two volunteer paramedics run intravenous lines into what is left of the wasting of his arms. Feeling a jolt from my head to my tailbone on his intrusions. He has known for months now, that the cancer had set up additional housing in his lungs and organs, paying brave indifference to its choice of locations. Often barley able to curl himself up in fetal position, as anecdotic sunshine streamed through his window. Having faltered for a second or two, the fur on the back of my dogs neck now stands up, a rumble erupting from her throat, as if a last warning as the ambulance drives off. My resolve crumbling just enough to further doubt my own perceptions, doubting my ability to have perceived the danger of his lack of breathing, early enough to have been able to save him. The ambulance now out of sight and sound. Following the scent out the door, the dog and I walk home, as the fragile structure of my mind further unravels chewing away at myself. It will not take me long to die by my own hands, as life all around me is abandoning. Feeling my own body rearrange itself, as a chunk of asphalt layers on my heart. My dog having fully known longer than any of us, from the scent of the infection deep within, looking deep into human eyes, that life's ocean was soon to wash away one of us from this isolated island.

Taking my grief to the most macabre level, brooding over the mystery of death, as my dog becomes my grieving partner. My dog having now taking up the fight with me, protecting me, in a way that is non negotiable. Leash in hand, we succumb to the horrors of the day, leaving the smell of death behind us, as we close the door to the cottage. I hold onto my sense of despair, as my dog tries to console me.

Something changes for me, in this instant of a moment, as a man suddenly appears out of the shadows and demands to walk with me. Are you there God, is it you? I beg for him to let the man live, just one more day, a few more days, a few more months, anything, for him not to die before dusk today. He is the one continual constant in my every waking day; I cannot bare to have that end. I begged for mercy brazenly. Survival at this point meant sacrificing a bit of my soul. I am prepared for the undoing, each begging of prayers a private act of contrition, escape and confrontation.

Helplessness begins to set in as my growing confusion takes center stage. My situation becoming ever more beyond my ability to control, even in small doses. Feeling as high and dry as the desert, needing air, I step outside. My foot giving out on the solid ice on the sidewalk, equilibrium now shot. Tilting sharply to one side, I crawl backwards in freezing temperatures to my house door. Believing now, that sticking to the venue of the stairs to the bedroom is ample enough trickery for me. Carefully choreographed defenses are not being able to keep up with the changes occurring in my body. The outer world demonstrating a direct and deliberate need to judge, thus which they do not understand.

Taking my position in the passenger seat, off to another round of silicone injection. Dark emotion swirls around my cockpit, as if someone is tap dancing on my head. The injection and discomfort fill me to my eyes. If misery loves company, then I am preparing for many guests, conceding little ground, fighting many loosing battles. Not needing to keep score, but I do, anyway.

Difficulties with my cognition, loosing trains of thought, errors in simplified spelling, increases my threshold of frustration with, well, just about anyone, other than the dog. Humiliation never swallows easily for me. Gazing through walls in my dreams pale and gaunt, I fall to a much needed sleep. Surgeries and injections fending themselves into considerable pain, always jump starting my emotions after the intrusion. They are solitary moments, feeling numb, but needing to survive. Surgeries aggressive, no path of least resistance for me, joining my body in a rest needed to heal.

Often falling into the shivering cold presence of my own mortality, as I lie in bed staring at the ceiling. The darkness of the night brings on the clamoring, as my heart drops to my feet, in recognition of needing to run somewhere, anywhere, away from here.

Cancer, in a heightened need, to hijack all of my brother's body, as lungs once again, are inflated, courtesy of a hospital medical team. In the morning he will be returned to the cottage, and then fall to the floor, as his shout out of pain hits the ceiling in a thunderous lion's roar. The heavy scent of

ghosts, his new live–in companions of each lung-
ful day, arriving early, staying late, leaving finger
marks on the light switch.

A football size tumor now pushes through his
back, having been channeled through his ribcage
for the passage. A tumor area pressed firmly on his
brain, creeping from behind the optic center.

Then there is the liver, pancreas, lungs, bones,
gallbladder, prostrate, bladder, all having been com-
promised as cancer's playground. Feeling the ten-
derness of his hands, the knowledge of his fear. His
willingness to still reach out, for the things that
keep him alive. Knowing you are going to die, do
thoughts scatter? What do you do after that? I wonder what a person can do after that, what else could
ever possibly matter? I think that any attempt at
happiness must be short lived. Aspirating, as if tiny
thoughts are being sucked out through a thin straw,
thinking about the cancer.

Heat overpowers me, every time I feel my heart
grow weak as I watch the even more profound limitations of his body. Devoid of conversation, the cottage grows still in the background. Antique clock
on the wall coated in a thin layer of nicotine, the
pendulum perched in silence, as the seepage of
time stands still.

God, can you hear me?

Tick, tick, tick... pendulum abruptly stops